BUZZKILL

One Man's Disorderly
Struggle with
Bipolar Disorder

Peter Goodman

Dedicated to my lovely daughter Madeline.
I hope this book will explain a lot of things when you are older.
I love you.

Special thanks to Constance Gordon for helping make this book possible.

Buzzkill
By: Peter Goodman

Table of Contents

The Big House

I could see myself getting shanked out on B-Yard or getting forced into a cell, while a plus-sized African American inmate named Detroit had his way with me as I lay face down on a cot, screaming into a pillow. I had watched enough TV to know that I could end up owing someone a favor if they kept me from getting "poked" in the chow line and then I'd be in debt to them forever. And when I couldn't keep up my payments of ramen noodles and sweet buns from the canteen anymore, my own cellie would be instructed to "put me down" by placing a plastic bag over my head while I was sleeping and choke me out. My heart felt like it was going to jump out of my rib cage. I was going to be locked in and I couldn't just walk right out. It was a process that took at least half an hour. I really needed one of my Lorazepam to calm my nerves, but I couldn't take drugs into the prison.

I told myself this was all silliness. I was at San Quentin as a volunteer to teach a college level course in communications to good-behavior inmates in their Prison University Project. I was not going to be teaching alone and guards were everywhere for my protection. I had spoken up as an inmate advocate all my life and now I was putting my beliefs into action. I was doing the work I had always wanted to do.

The guard at the front gates name tag simply said "Brick." He looked like a Brick. With classic horseshoe pattern baldness, I couldn't help think he was a perfect candidate for the Bosley hair replacement system. But he didn't seem overly concerned with his appearance. Six feet tall, red faced, stocky, and an oversized gun in his holster, just to make sure he didn't miss. He looked like if you crossed him he'd drop down to one knee, whip out his firearm, close one eye and shoot you in the leg as you ran toward the visitor's parking lot for safety. When he was born his parents just took one look at him and in unison said, "We'll call him Brick." He probably pissed concrete blocks and didn't mind the pain. America is number one. Let's bomb New Zealand. The Innocence Project? None of them are innocent! I was sure he hated me with my long hair and razor stubble.

The smallest infraction and he would not let you teach that night, and you couldn't wear blue because that's the color the prisoners wore. Women couldn't show bra straps or wear pants that would possibly expose their panties when they bent over. No open-toed or heeled shoes because the prisoners would be jealous of your pedicure. And if Brick just didn't like you, he'd *find* a reason to not let you in. After all, we were giving these criminals a free education and his kids had to pay for one. We were just a bunch of hippies from Berkeley and San Francisco. He probably yearned for the days of chain gangs and one-man stand-up sweatboxes for those good ole boys that "had a little jack rabbit in em'." I thought when he watched the movie *Cool Hand Luke* he probably rooted for the guards.

The first night, my group of teachers and I had made it through Brick's gate first. At the next gate we'd be searched with a metal detector and face a possible pat down. I started to obsess. What if someone accidentally planted drugs on me? Maybe they slipped hash into my pockets or shoved a kilo of cocaine up my ass when I wasn't paying attention? Was I going to have to bend over and cough? Would I be frisked? What if they found the drugs and hauled me right off to strip a cell, which is a cell with nothing in it but a bed, sink and toilet? These irrational thoughts raced through my mind with complete validity. Maybe this wasn't such a good idea. Who voluntarily walks into San Quentin? What if I had to take a urine test? I smoked pot every night. I'd stain the specimen cup with the amount of THC in my body.

However, I was already inside the first gate. At the second gate was a guard with a metal detector. "Oh god," I thought. I suddenly remembered I had a Lorazepam pill in a little piece of tin foil in my front pant pocket for an emergency panic attack. Like the one I had in San Diego touring an aircraft carrier with my boss while at a PBS convention. I would have jumped overboard without it. In prison I'd have to go over the wall and they'd probably shoot me. God, I hoped they didn't find that little pill.

But the metal detector came up clean. I also got an infrared stamp on my wrist that said "pass." I was told not to wash it off. That night I guarded it with my life against any kind of liquid. I became terrified that I might start sweating it off. I tried to remember if I was a wrist sweater or just prone to the pit schvitz.

All this time I was clasping my butt cheeks as tightly as possible so the kilo of coke would not slip out of my ass and down my pant leg. I was sure somebody made me a mule without me knowing it. I decided if the cocaine did slip out, I'd kick it over to the nearest, meanest-looking inmate and ask what was in the funny wrapper by his foot.

Next we were locked between two barred doors called a sally port and waited to be let into the next part of the prison. We were essentially locked in ourselves. There were about ten of us volunteers in there. I was just about to ask if anyone had a tattoo gun when they released us into the outer yard. It was actually very well landscaped. I grew a little more relaxed until I saw the huge memorial for all the San Quentin guards that were killed in the line of duty. That's all I needed to see. If guards can get killed, what about unarmed volunteer teachers? Was I a sitting duck?

Walking to the education building took us right into the main yard loaded with convicts dressed in blue. I had seen this yard countless times on TV and here I was, alone with a bunch of unarmed civilians walking amongst killers, thieves and rapists. Some of them said "hello" and others just looked us over. The whole yard was divided by race and I was informed that the whites got the bottom of the barrel when it came to prison yard real estate. The Mexicans were king of the roost. Being white as the moon, I began to feel very vulnerable. My long hair was definitely drawing attention. It felt like everyone was looking me up and down. I almost forgot how to walk.

There were also rows of stainless steel toilets right out in the open. If a prisoner had to take a shit, they did it in front of the whole yard. To me this was the ultimate degradation. I pictured myself sitting on one making the bathroom face while inmates walked by and snickered. I hoped that if I had to use the facilities that night, I wouldn't have to go out in the yard while all the volunteer teachers saw me crouching on a dirty cold metal exposed latrine.

Inside the education building my teaching partner and I had to sign in again and finally got to set up our classroom. I wanted to call my girl-friend and tell her everything I had seen but couldn't. No cell phones allowed. I wanted to take the Lorazepam to calm down and then I real-ized it wasn't in my pocket anymore. I panicked. It must have fallen out. So the fact of the matter was I would be behind the yellowing Spanish castle-like walls of San Quentin for the next two-plus hours and I had to deal with only the psychotropic drugs that were already in my system. It would be damn hard to get someone to save me if I fell apart. Even then it would take at least half an hour to process-out through all the security gates.

So then all I could think about was what if my medication stopped working? What if I got so depressed and panicked that I fell to the floor in a huddled mass of hysterical tears? What if I went manic and couldn't slow myself down and gave the convicts a freak show? What if? What if? I was essentially incarcerated for the moment. Maybe this wasn't something a bipolar II could handle? Did I finally bite off more than I could chew? Would my quest to always push the limits of my illness and live in the nor-mal world finally prove more than I could handle? Was this big buzz I had for prison reform going to throw me over the edge and finally beat me down to a paranoid shut-in, living on disability for the rest of my life? Or, at the very least would I end up in the lollipop factory for a few weeks?

And what the fuck made me think I could teach? I wasn't a teacher. I hated school. True, I was experienced in mass media and media sales. I'd guessed I was going to be "the color man" in what I figured would be a series of boring lectures. Kind of like the sports announcer who gives the trivia while the other guy just calls the plays. Yes, my teaching part-ner and I had a syllabus and planned each class. But when a bunch of men in blue with the word "prisoner" in orange written down their pant legs entered the room, all I wanted to say was, "Gee guys, I'm really sorry you're in here," like it was my fault or something.

And suddenly we were surrounded by the men in blue. Blacks on one side of the room and whites on the other. But everyone wore their uniforms a little differently. Some shirts neat and tucked in. Some out and sloppy. Some had what looked like blue hospital scrubs on. Others had button down blue tops. A few guys had pristine white tennis shoes. A few wore old leather shoes. One had headphones on so you couldn't be exactly sure what he was hearing. I wondered if he did this on purpose? Others carried clear bottles of some kind of red juice. Many of the guys had sunglasses on, which they slid to the top of their heads when they entered the classroom. These men were determined to reject the forced uniformity and individualize themselves in any way possible. And they did the same with their hair: braids, shaved heads, goatees, perfectly groomed moustaches, anything to be individuals. Uniform ensembles and hair were all they had to work with, so they got very creative.

As everyone sat quietly and waited for class to start, I realized I didn't know how to talk to these men. I had twelve convicts waiting to see what I was all about, but we were instructed in orientation not to say or ask anything too personal. So all there was to talk about was the class. And thinking of myself as a teacher was just a big farce; thinking of myself in any position of authority amused me. I didn't think they'd take me too seriously if they knew about the suicide attempts, stays in the mental ward, embarrassing manic behavior, obsessive compulsions and severe depression, where I'd sit in the shower bawling my eyes out uncontrollably, begging for someone to kill me.

But my partner just started teaching and when she threw the ball in my court I just began talking. I was nervous at first, but I decided if I acted like a teacher everyone would think I was a teacher. So I taught. Instead of trying to teach out of the book, I let her do that and then linked her statements to something they could relate to in the news or from their lives in prison, like paralleling rules of communication in a small office setting to communicating with a small group of guys on their cell tiers. It seemed to make it easier for them to understand the concepts. Slowly, as I grew more comfortable, the imaginary kilo of cocaine disappeared from my ass.

After a while I got to know the men as individuals. As a whole they generally worked hard on every activity and assignment. Through class and helping them with papers and projects one-on-one I learned what put them in prison, how long they were in for, if they were ever getting out and why they wanted to better themselves with an education.

A big, muscular middle-aged black man named Erik ran men's self-esteem groups and counseled teens inside San Quentin. He wanted to learn how to become a better speaker so he could be a more effective facilitator and mentor. I'd never met someone so involved with social programs.

A tall, lanky, fashionably bespectacled young guy called Shytown was appealing his forty-five years to life sentence and after thirteen years was making some serious headway with the California Supreme Court. He wanted to learn to communicate better when he represented himself in front of the judge.

Daryl, a tall, thin, grey-haired man had been incarcerated since he was eighteen. He was now in his fifties and going in front of the parole board again. He felt getting an education, especially learning to be a better communicator, would help him gain his freedom.

TJ was tragic. A forty-year-old man from Alabama serving a life sentence. Shy, sensitive and secretly smart, he tried to raise his daughter from a jail cell. He grew up dirt poor and getting a college education was something he probably never thought could happen for him. The shame of it was that it had to happen in prison.

Then there was Tokyo. Good looking, smart, articulate and intelligent. Came to San Quentin at fifteen to serve a life sentence. Now he was twenty-eight. He regretted what he had done and probably would have been wildly successful at whatever he touched in the real world. Simply a wasted life. But unbelievably, he didn't appear bitter.

I think I learned more from the inmates than they learned from me. True, most of them committed the crimes they were incarcerated for. They would tell you that themselves. However, I doubt that seventy-five percent of the sentences were fair. Most of them were from throw-away-the-key judges spurred on by reactionary California lawmakers trying to showboat for their constituents.

What I learned from the inmates was patience. If a man could sit in a tiny, hot, two-man cell for thirty-five years, constantly passed over by the parole board for ridiculous reasons, be disrespected by guards, eat food prepared by men with a vengeance, while year after year family abandons him or dies off, and still remain philosophical with a glimmer of hope; then I could learn to withstand the discomfort of depression, go about my daily responsibilities and be hopeful that it would pass.

Leaving San Quentin that evening I was much calmer, partly because I was going home and partly because the experience wasn't at all what I had imagined. But it still felt nice walking through the various check points, showing my ID and signing myself out three different times. And when I got to my car in the visitor's parking lot without being shot in the leg by Brick, it felt wonderful to be swaddled in the luxurious pleather seats of my Mustang as I gunned it toward the freeway back to nearby San Francisco. As I sped toward the Bay Bridge I thought of the men who weren't going home that evening and my heart suddenly felt very heavy.

Prison is a cesspool and there are some pretty evil people within its walls. However, you'd be surprised how many of them are not. But these guys still have to live among this filth for years, sometimes a lifetime. They wash their clothes in toilets. Defecate in commodes two inches from their cellmate's heads. Eat food your dog wouldn't touch. Spend days locked in six- by nine-foot cells with nothing to do but count the cracks on the walls, while having no idea what is going on with their cases and often being represented by horrendous state-provided counsel. Surely I can use some of their strength to survive when my bipolar-depression and anxiety is at its worst.

Unfortunately, I didn't have this experience until later in life. I hadn't seen the big picture until visiting the big house, which in a way helped me put my own house in order.

Fun with Pharmaceuticals

Have you ever met a holistic health fanatic? My ex-wife Debra's father was a transcendental meditation devotee and longtime follower of the Maharishi, both his teachings and his costly pre-packaged holistic products. For years he was sending Debra this paste that looked and tasted like melted black licorice. She was directed to eat a spoonful twice a day lest her health decline and she eventually drop dead. So she religiously chocked down this goo to protect herself from sickness and generally improve her overall health.

One day after living together in our pre-marital years I told her I thought this paste-like substance was a waste of money. I asked her to try and get her father to stop sending it, but he feared for a decline in her health. He kept sending it and she kept taking it so as not to waste his money. I thought this was twisted logic, but I also felt it was because she did not want to upset her father. The man loved the goo.

Finally I couldn't take it anymore. Witnessing her spoon this stuff out when I knew it was a scam infuriated me. Watching her eat it reminded me of a dog trying to eat peanut butter, smacking its lips and struggling to swallow. I became convinced the Maharishi was nothing more than a vitamin supplement distributor. After the 1970s he probably lost a lot of followers when they came out of their drug-induced comas so he had to find a new stream of income, so he literally went back to his *roots* with health products.

At last I reminded Debra that while taking this concoction she developed a brain tumor that had to be surgically removed in a major operation. I told her she couldn't deny that *either the mush didn't work,* or *it didn't work for everyone.* Either way it was a waste of time for her to keep taking it because it was obviously ineffective in her immune system. She finally saw the irony in it and gave up the gook, much to her father's dismay.

But the licorice-tasting gunk is in a sense like psychotropic drugs given for bipolar disorders. Generally, a bipolar disorder is when an individual cannot control moods and suffers from uncontrollable highs and lows. Although psychotropic drugs have been definitively proven to work, the same drugs do not work on each individual. Plus, each individual can only tolerate a specific dosage.

I was not diagnosed with bipolar disorder until my early thirties. In my early twenties I was said to have severe depression, which is a *unipolar* disorder. So the litany of drugs tested on me like a lab rat were antidepressants. Their purpose was to keep me from my deep bouts of depression. Nobody had been concerned that while taking these medications I'd suddenly become amped up like a mop top teenager, wildly dancing to some head banging garage rock on American Bandstand in the late 1960s. The doctors just thought the medication was working.

Currently diagnosed as bipolar, I take 600 mg of Seroquel in the evening or else I cannot sleep on my own. Seroquel was an antipsychotic but became treated off-label, or prescribed by doctors for something other than its intended use, as a bipolar drug. For those who cannot tolerate Seroquel, even a 20 mg dose makes them extremely sleepy and disoriented. For people like me, an elephant dose of 600 mg allows me to sleep and function normally the next day. Incredibly, others may need more than 600 mg. That Herculean dose is given with the gun used to shoot big game.

A psychotropic drug is a mood-altering compound used to treat the bipolar condition by manipulating dopamine in the brain, which affects mood. Dopamine infringes upon norepinephrine, which controls bursts of energy, also affecting mood. This is a simplified explanation of how psychotropic drugs work.

Sure, some doctors have done elaborate brain scans assigning each chemical in the brain a color. They claim they can predict which chemical is lacking and then make a targeted recommendation on what drugs can be used to correct the deficiencies. But it's all a pile of Maharishi mush at this point. Very experimental.

All bipolar sufferers have gone through periods where a medication introduction or change is necessary. Having the wrong medication in your system can be even more traumatic than taking nothing at all. And, stopping one medication to try another can cause withdrawal symptoms the likes of giving up heroine. Except that it's a lot cooler to give up heroine than it is to get off the Effexor antidepressant extended-release capsules.

I've spent weeks in utter misery as the psychiatrist tried different drugs on me to ease my depression or mania, weaning me off one and onto another. In the interim I often found myself sitting in the bathtub with the shower trickling down on me, crying until I was hyperventilating, wishing I were dead. The depression was bottomless but my body wouldn't slow down or allow me to even sit quietly or sleep a little. It was like there were swarms of ants scratching me, making me itch and very annoyingly scurrying through my veins. There is no way out of this state except suicide or faith in my doctor finding the right drug, dosage or combination of drugs. I fear this condition more than anything in the world. I'd rather be dead.

If you are able to function during a medication withdrawal, adjustment or change, it's a horrible existence. You walk through your daily life with the desire for suicide constantly encroaching upon every attempt to distract yourself. All you can do is hope nobody can tell your hands are shaking or your voice is quivering. You pray people don't realize you are ready to cry at the drop of a hat. You think to yourself, "Just hold it together a little longer and then you can go home and fall apart." Nothing can possibly divert your attention. You constantly fight the urge to call your doctor and scream, "Do you know what the fuck I am going through? Get off the goddamn tennis court and fix me!"

Psychiatrists are basically playing roulette with medications to treat bipolar illness. Many try what they have experience with or what *The Physician's Desk Reference* prescribes, which was more conservative with its treatments than an eighty-five-year-old lady in Iowa driving her 1968 Chrysler Newport to bible study on a Sunday. But it's all hit or miss.

About twenty years ago there was a big breakthrough on the psycho-tropic drug front. Since a major symptom of bipolar illness is severe depression, almost all patients were given an antidepressant. The problem was that bipolar by definition means two poles: depression and mania. The antidepressant cured the depression but frequently sent patients into mania. Guys were driving to work in Toyotas and came home in Corvettes, having quit their jobs to start their own consulting firms, totally freaking out their wives and girlfriends.

Consequently, doctors also started prescribing drugs called mood stabilizers to bipolars taking antidepressants. Mood stabilizers are kind of like the governors they put on school buses to keep the drivers from drag racing. Most can't go over fifty miles per hour.

Mood stabilizers do the same thing. If the antidepressant tries to take you too high, it acts as a limiter. And if you go too low, it keeps you from crashing. Yes, it does stabilize your mood, but it can also make you feel like you are simply observing life through a telescope and not actually living it. However, today's psychiatrists will not prescribe anti-depressants to a bipolar patient without a mood stabilizer. God forbid we are elated with our illness. Then everyone would want to be bipolar.

Then there is the best part about taking psychotropic drugs: the side effects. These are the annoying physical ailments caused by the medica-tion bipolars often silently suffer with in order to pay the cost for feeling "blah." Yes, even if the drugs are not working that well, many doctors consider "blah" an acceptable outcome, whether the patient thinks so or not. I think a lot of psychiatrists feel they are doing well if a patient sim-ply doesn't commit suicide. Can you imagine a dermatologist bragging about their successful career because they never lost a patient to acne?

Common side effects are weight gain, shaking hands, dizziness, sex-ual dysfunction, constipation, blurred vision, short-term memory loss, dry mouth and extreme sleepiness. I have had all of these at one time or another, sometimes in combination. If anybody tells you that psy-chotropic drugs are nonsense, ask, "Who would put up with these side effects if the drugs do not make a significant difference in their mood and ability to function?"

Some of the older psychotropic drugs are famous for multiple side effects, like the antidepressant Elavil which was one of the first to come out in the late 1950s. The drug took a shotgun approach to depression. Unlike today's drugs that work on select brain receptors, Elavil took them all out. It also dulled your sex drive to the point of "why bother," gave you irritable bowel syndrome, sucked all the saliva out of your mouth so you spoke with a lisp and made you gain enough weight that you never would take your shirt off in public again.

Newer antidepressants like Prozac, Cymbalta, Effexor and the like are better at pinpointing the source of depression in the brain and have fewer side effects. But I have never heard of an antidepressant with no drawbacks. If you are taking a psychotropic drug, you are going to have to deal with some sort of discomfort. Nobody gets a free ride.

I have had a long history with psychotropic medications. It's basically been a big guessing game of what will work and how much to take. Apparently what is therapeutic for me has no real rhyme or reason. And my metabolism is so fast I have to take very large doses of them.

However, I have decided I'd rather my shaky hands occasionally dump coffee on my shirt and have people speak slower to me because they think I'm "retarded" due to my dry mouth than go without the drugs. I know without drugs I will die. And it does scare me to think without these annoyingly colorful pills and capsules I cease to function.

But then I'm glad I wasn't born in 1948 where I'd be in a mental institution wearing a strait jacket and getting a lobotomy to cure my depression. That's what happened to people like me back then. Now I slowly lobotomize myself by taking Topamax as a mood stabilizer, allowing it to eat away at my short-term memory ever so slowly, hoping I retain just enough so I can at least find my car in the supermarket parking lot.

I often wonder if the guy sitting next to me at the lunch counter in my favorite diner has any idea of what I have to do and tolerate just to function enough to sit there with him? He is enjoying his BLT and maybe thinking about what he is going to do on the weekend. I'm sitting there worried about the fact I am starting to feel jumpy and depressed at the same time, called a "mixed state," from which I often suffer. I want to take my medication then, even if it's a little too early. However, I know it makes me nauseated so maybe I should eat first, because I probably won't want food for the rest of the day after taking it. I think, "God, does my fucking stomach hurt. I'm so bloated I feel like William Shatner in those Priceline television commercials. And my mouth is so dry I can't wait until the waitress brings me my iced tea. Does anyone notice my hand shaking as I pick up my menu?" I nervously wonder if I will be in a mixed state for the rest of the day. "I hope not, I have work to do back at the office."

The man sitting next to me takes another big bite of his BLT.

Maniac Braniac

If you see someone with a dry mouth, sweating profusely and moving very slowly, do you not surmise they are dehydrated and rush to get them some water and probably to a hospital as soon as possible? Or do you have a five-hour conversation with them about how it feels to be thirsty, browbeat them about what they did to let themselves get this way, tell them how they could have done things differently, give them exercises to help prevent being thirsty in the future, tell them not to think about it and then wait until they are near death before making a doctor's appointment to have their medical condition evaluated?

Meet my mother. This is how she let me live for years before finally getting me help for the mental illness she had been struggling with all her life. She thought it'd leave her exposed to admit I had serious psychiatric issues that in many ways mirrored hers. And in my family nobody ever fessed up to what was really wrong. When my alcoholic stepfather fell off the commuter train in Philadelphia, ripping his left ear almost clean off his head, he sued the city for unsafe trains. As for his drunkenness? He's allergic to alcohol! Some people get hives. He gets drunk.

My mother reminds me of a goat because when you look into her eyes she has that same vacant stare. And, her voice is extremely annoying and repetitive like a goat "bahhhing," following you around a petting zoo trying to get you to feed her. Except my mother feeds on getting you to admit you are a mess, without ever admitting that she is the least bit warped. It makes her feel better about herself. "Peter, when are you going to talk to your doctor about upping your medications? You don't look well. Peter, when are you going to talk to your doctor about upping your medications? You don't look well. Peter, when are you going to talk to your doctor about upping your medications? You don't look well. Bahhhh."

The only difference between her and a real goat is that every time I see my mother her hair grows taller and taller and redder and redder, not thicker and whiter. And each time I see her she asks, "Do you notice something different about my hair?" One time my brother told her, "Yeah mom, it looks like it's ready to catch fire."

The funniest thing about her is that she thinks she is a "woman of privilege" and looks down on everyone else as proletariats. As she shuffles down the streets of Philadelphia, mumbling from being overmedicated with the fiery red hair and misfired red lipstick, she comments on the way everyone else is dressed, walking and talking. And all black people are her servants. Probably because her middle class family residing in a small four-bedroom Philadelphia row house always had a live-in maid. All she had to do was ring a bell for service. So now if she needs help with anything, she just looks for a black person. Hail a cab? Move some furniture? Fix her car? Find a black person. As her father would say, "They're used to it. They like doing this kind of thing."

So I'm entering my second freshman year, this time at Temple University in Philadelphia. This is where I wanted to go in the first place. I preferred a school located in a war zone like North Philadelphia. Rolling hills and green grass bored the hell out of me. My first freshman year was at the University of Delaware. My parents were divorced for years and I was living with my dad, who wanted me to have a *real* college experience. He felt Temple was a city school and all I'd do was run wild. To this day he thinks every time my brother or I walk out the door of our respective homes we are running wild in some fashion. Especially if spending money is involved. When I started dating after my divorce he actually got mad at me because he felt it was too expensive and I was running wild.

However, "Dela-Where?" did not work out past midway into the second semester. Just like in high school, I couldn't focus in classes or get myself to sit down and really study. I tried so hard, but I couldn't. And I was barely skating by, which was making me feel even more miserable, inferior to other students and guilty for wasting my student loan money. Plus they put me in a dorm room with a sixteen-year-old prodigy. Why not just give me a speech impediment and a limp while they were at it? All my life I felt like I always drew the short straw. Oh, woe is me!

Also, at this point I had not been to a psychiatrist for any kind of evaluation whatsoever. I was half firecracker and half big lump of shit hibernating in bed under a pile of blankets. trying to sleep the depression away.

And I detested living in the dorm. The Spartan light blue cement block walls and institutional green speckled tile floors in my room depressed me. I felt like I was living in a storage closet. Standing in line and eating in a huge dining hall like I was in the Army depressed me. Having to take classes and live with the same annoying people depressed me. The walk through the green middle of nowhere campus to my classes depressed me. I honestly felt like I had been sent to some sort of institution as a punishment.

It reminded me of when I was forced go to overnight camp for three summers in a row in the mid-seventies because my parents wanted me to learn to like sports, make more Jewish friends and enjoy it as much as they had when they were clean cut Jewish kids in the late fifties and early sixties. Every year I would cry for the first week, call my parents and beg to come home. I hated the dirty bunks, shit-clogged toilets, decrepit sagging metal beds, forced participation in sports, practical jokes played on me and lying down every night next to the very kids who routinely dealt them out. Even the girls made fun of me. I had no confidence and it showed. On top of that the sunlight depressed me, the strange placement of linoleum on the dining hall tables depressed me, the dusty trail leading to the bunks depressed me and the watered down drink served with every meal they called "bug juice" depressed me.

So the University of Delaware was making me feel just like I did in overnight camp. But this time when I cried I was allowed to go home. Probably because I had a car. However, breaking my foot and getting mono didn't hurt. So when I went home for a weekend to my dad's to show him my war wounds I decided not to go back. And one of the major standup things he did for me in my life was let me drop out and stay with him for the summer to recuperate. This is a man who uses both sides of the toilet paper to get the most out of it, and he was letting me throw away a semester of college. Plus he supported me for the entire summer, although I really couldn't work with mono. Maybe he felt guilty for forcing me to go to Delaware in the first place. However, I was sick, depressed and twisted up inside and really needed help that summer. My father really came through for me and made things a lot less stressful.

But entering Temple University that fall was great. I loved Philadelphia, my student apartment, my four roommates and classes. We went to parties, threw eggs and fried chicken at cars driving down 13th Street from our balcony and watched the news every night to see what serial killer was arrested while trying to hide out on our campus.

Plus I turned into a study fiend. I went to every class and took copious notes. I spent hours every night in the library forcing myself to copy and recopy outlines I made from books and lectures, thus committing them to memory. If I had ten spare minutes, I'd squeeze in a chapter I needed to read in one of my classes. I studied all day Saturday and Sunday. I'd end dates early because I felt guilty for not studying enough. I was also getting mostly A's with a few B's here and there.

For the first time in my life I was doing well academically. I wasn't stupid. I taught myself to study and could not only pass my classes, but I could master them. People were coming to *me* for help!

But as usual, what should have been a good thing threatened to be my demise. It's like when a guy first learns about masturbating. Suddenly masturbating as many times a day as humanly possible is the only thing that matters. Not only does it feel good, but it makes you feel like a man. Some guys start replacing other activities in their life with masturbating. "To hell with the soccer team and Eagle Scouts. I have a penis that needs attention!"

Well, that's how I became about college. To hell with going out all night to parties. I had a brain I had just discovered. And it needed attention! For the first time in my life I felt like a student.

Unbeknownst to me, it was obvious to my mother what was wrong. For how long, I don't know. I was monomaniacal about my studies. I was hysterical about doing everything exactly the same as the semester before so I wouldn't jinx myself. I had a terrible fear of the jinx. I wasn't depressed but my insides were all twisted up in anxiety and excitement. I was also smoking a lot of cigarettes, I'd guess about two packs of Marlboros a day. I had been smoking regularly since I was thirteen, but never this much. I was beginning to feel unhealthy, like a fat man selling insurance. I wasn't running much anymore, which was my favorite exercise, and my body felt like it might be breaking down as well. But I had to keep studying.

One Saturday night my grandparents had one of their gala dinners for the family at a downtown Philadelphia restaurant to celebrate the 49th anniversary of something. As a side note, we never got to celebrate the 50th anniversary of anything because my grandfather would get so worked up the day before, he'd collapse and have to be rushed to the hospital, canceling the festivities.

I'd usually get loaded with my brother and have a pretty good time making fun of our relatives and our stepfather's high waistline at these things, but instead I was sitting with everyone in the cocktail lounge having a vodka tonic and starting on my second pack of "mules" for the day. My mother had sat down next to me and said I didn't seem right and asked what was wrong. Back then you could still understand what she was saying, before the medication made her sound like a female version of Grady from *Sanford and Son*.

"I feel all wound up and exhausted at the same time. Like I'm about to fall on my face but my mind is racing too much. I'm up and down all at once." I didn't know how else to describe it. "It's like I want to get off this ride."

"Bahhhh, I want to take you to my doctor for an appointment. I want to take you to my doctor for an appointment. I want to take you to my doctor for an appointment. He can help you I think. I have been watching you. You're a lot like me."

God, I hoped not. I wasn't sure what she was talking about. But I didn't care. I wanted to feel better. I knew she always saw a lot of doctors and that she ended up in the hospital for "a rest" now and then, so I figured it had to do with a physical problem I might have inherited. Maybe I needed vitamins? I just certainly hoped I wasn't going to end up like her. Now that worried me to no end.

"Okay, Mom. Let me know when." I needed some kind of relief and I was open to trying anything. I felt like I was studying myself to death.

I left the party early that night to start writing a term paper.

The Rockford Files

I have been obsessed with *The Rockford Files* since I first saw my mother watching the show in what I guess must have been 1974, and have never stopped loving James Garner and the cast of characters since then. In 2008, thirty-four years later, I even got personalized California license plates on my Mustang that nearly matched the California plates on Jim Rockford's bronze Firebird Esprit as closely as possible. The actual OKG 853 plate is still taken.

The Rockford Files have meant different things to me at different times. As an eight-year-old boy in Bethlehem, Pennsylvania, Jim Rockford was everything I wanted to be: a private investigator living in Los Angeles, traveling around its exotic cities like Malibu, Santa Monica and Beverly Hills, screaming up and down the Pacific Coast Highway in that bronze Firebird "following up on a hunch." And I didn't care if "I caught a federal beef" or got roughed up outside my trailer. I even wished my dad looked like a grizzly old fisherman and I could start calling him "Rocky," like Jim's dad.

Bethlehem's exciting locales included Hellertown, Trexlertown and Macungie. And instead of getting to be a big time private eye I was relinquished to a tiny private Christian school where I was one of two Jews, not very popular, and a poor student with terrible impulse control, making me a pathetic class clown who never knew when to stop. Moreover, no matter how many cases I tried to take on, I could never convince anyone I was a private eye. And the only thing I got to ride around in was a 1973 Mercury station wagon up and down Schoenersville Road. Did I mention it was a Marquis Colony Park, Mercury's top of the line wagon? I know I mentioned it to James Garner when I sent him a fan letter.

In those days my life revolved around Friday nights at 9:00 P.M. watching *The Rockford Files* on CBS Television. The largest punishment in the world that my parents could dole out was not letting me watch. And my mother used this power to her absolute merriment. Even if I had done nothing wrong she would engage me in a conversation until 8:59 P.M. on a Friday night until she decided to release me to watch my program. Or she'd suddenly decide to punish me, not let me watch the program and banish me to my room for the evening. And if I tried to reason with her she'd drag me into my room with a wild and spastic flurry of kicking and hitting. Sometimes out of frustration I would scream that I hated her from behind my closed door. In she'd come and take a few more slaps at me with an open hand at whatever part of my face I couldn't cover. All the time she had the vacant look in her eyes like the goats at the petting zoo.

The Friday anxiety would be unbearable. Soon she began using Friday against me all week. It got to the point that I couldn't wait for summer reruns. Would I watch *The Rockford Files* and get my one hour of escape a week? Or would my mother play with me to watch my anxiety level rise? Would I do something to slip up and be sent to solitary? Would I provoke her physical frustration that night? Was she taking things out on me because on Fridays my dad always stayed out until 4:00 A.M.?

I remember in the spring of 1980 my mother, brother and I were living in an apartment in Philadelphia and I started hitting back. I don't remember the reason for the altercation. There was always something. She was swinging at me spastically with a wire hairbrush in the kitchen, a preferred implement because it left marks. Finally I immobilized her hairbrush arm and smacked her hard across the face with my hand.

"This one is for all the time you didn't let me watch *The Rockford Files*, you bitch," I screamed and cackled at the same time. It just kind of came out. Coincidentally, the show had gone off the air that year.

She stopped for a moment and looked at me like I had lost my mind. It made me laugh like a madman. Then she just started screaming and trying to swing at me again, "I am your mother! I am your mother! I am your mother! You will not speak to me like that!" This was a mantra of hers.

"Those days are over, bitch," I said, pushing her into the stove as I backed out the kitchen screen door and down the fire exit steps to the ground floor of the apartment building. Although at that time we probably hated each other, we were sharing the exact same adrenaline rush. I kind of liked it. Especially how it evened up the balance of power.

As a kid I had always prayed this might happen one day, but when it finally came to fruition I was ecstatic. I was completely "chulo" walking down the street to my friend Joe's, Marlboro hanging out of my mouth, bandana out of my back pocket and long blond rat's nest of hair waiving in the wind. "Teenage wasteland, baby," I thought to myself. These were the words, minus the baby, to a popular Who song at the time called "Baba O'Reilly." My druggie friends and I realized it was written specifically for our generation as a call to revolution against authority.

And what was my dad doing out until 4am every Friday? He just drove to bars far enough away from Bethlehem where nobody else would recognize him relaxing and socializing away from my mother. A chance to be someone else besides that lawyer married to the lunatic lady from Philadelphia. Maybe even just to be with another woman who didn't make him want to slit his wrists every time she opened her mouth. It was no picnic being married to my mother. Her obsessive-compulsive disorder, constant badgering and criticism about every single thing were making him go insane.

Don't get me wrong, my dad had a temper and it didn't help matters. He could yell so loud it would make the doorbell chimes ring on their own. And I once saw him smack my brother Andy so hard on the ass he was propelled up an entire flight of stairs. I later learned it was because he had not unrolled the toilet paper correctly from the roller, giving it a sloppy appearance. It would have been kind of cool to watch if I didn't feel so bad for my brother. I think I saw a jet stream.

Or, I'd be sitting at the dinner table, accidentally chewing with my mouth open as kids sometimes do, and my father's hand would come out of nowhere and crack me upside my head so hard I'd sometimes fall off my chair. I looked like a prizefighter catching a knockout blow in slow motion, my eyes squinting shut, swollen cheeks involuntarily spurting out food as I almost crashed to the floor and the referee counted me out. When he caught me off guard I'd actually be stunned momentarily.

The fact of the matter was, he hit hard enough to leave marks, he did it a lot and he was basically a difficult human being to be around while married to my mother. He just couldn't hide his unhappiness and he used any little infraction of the rules to take it out on my brother and me.

I think he was so miserable with my mother that he subconsciously made sure my brother and I were miserable, too. Everything bothered him. Eating like a kid at the dinner table, not holding our utensils properly, walking too hard up the steps causing the carpet to wear unevenly and getting in and out of the car while accidentally scraping the inside of the door with our shoes set him off. However, I don't think he understood what he was doing or could even help himself if he did. And I think it was really hard for him to have a son like me with poor vision, poor coordination and emotional self-control issues that sometimes embarrassed him in public.

I'd laugh at the wrong times, say the wrong things and became overcome by emotion if my socks didn't match. Plus I had his thick glasses, which probably made him feel guilty for passing poor eyesight along. However, it wasn't his fault. I was born with a completely different condition called nystagmus, which gave me poor vision and made my eyes uncontrollably shift back and forth. I just wasn't the all-American, sports loving, cute little bastard he had expected his boy to be. I must have been a real disappointment on some level, although I don't think he'd ever say it.

So there I was, the farthest thing from Jim Rockford as anyone could be and I knew it. I was acutely aware that I hated everything about Bethlehem, Pennsylvania: its boring landscape, small town mentality constantly striving to be a big town, slap-happy parents and a no-frills life style. But it affected me so deeply I could never stop thinking about the sadness it brought on. I couldn't stand looking out my window and seeing what wasn't there, looking around my house and seeing it more as a prison with parents whose job, as I perceived it, was to hold me back.

To top it off I had anxiety about everything. I woke up every morning terrified that Lane Zabrisky, a minister's son, was going to stab me repeatedly with thorns at the bus stop. Once on the bus, I wondered who would be making fun of me for being Jewish in a school full of kids whose families came over on the Mayflower. While at school, nobody wanted to talk to me. I was the kid with the shifty eyes, thick glasses and problems paying attention in class because he was secretly wishing Jim Rockford's bronze Firebird would appear out of nowhere and take him away from it all.

I was always behind at school and could never read the blackboard, no matter how far up in class I sat. Consequently, I did not understand what was being taught and spent my days terrified I'd be called on in class to answer something. Frequently I'd become class clown out of boredom and be ejected from the room, relegated to standing in the hall. When kids walked by and saw me standing there the embarrassment was unbearable. I wanted to melt into the floor. "There's that Jew-boy goof-off Peter Goodman out in the hall again. What did he do this time?"

Then I was afraid, if I survived the bus ride home, my parents were going to find out about my time in the hallway with a call from the teacher. And if not, what kind of drama would unfold that evening anyway? I hated life. It got to the point where I didn't know what I hated more, home or school. I felt wound up and exhausted inside at the same time. I always wanted to cry but I couldn't find the tears.

Was this an unidentified bipolar disorder I was too young to make sense of? Had doctors even formally classified the disease in those days? I later thought back to the time I began treatment in my early twenties, mistakenly medicated for unipolar disorder. I was not treated for the dramatic mood swings of bipolar. When correctly diagnosed and treated for bipolar disorder it was almost ten years after that! I had been suffering from this thing for over a third of my life until I finally got the right help. I was miserable.

To top things off, I had Hebrew school on Tuesday and Thursday afternoons and Saturday mornings. This was a place where I could be told I was a loser in a language I did not even understand, Hebrew. Ah, the icing on the cake. And my parents, who were so keen on being good Jews, did not keep a Jewish household so I knew absolutely nothing compared to the other kids. At times I hated the Jews more than the Pilgrims with whom I attended regular school. This was pure torture, school after school.

The kid who saved me was my friend since kindergarten, Steve Goldstein. He knew all about being a good Jew, he just didn't care. We went to different grade schools but he was my closest confidante in Hebrew school and out. He was ahead of his time and later in life I'd realize he was probably one of the most intelligent people I ever knew.

At ten-years-old, Steve put Hebrew school into perspective for me. "Pete, it's not real school. Flunking out won't keep you from getting into a good college or something. You can't even really flunk out anyway. We can do whatever we want as long as our parents pay their dues to the temple."

Slowly, Steve brought me along in the world, breaking down many of my fears. At eleven he showed during the most holy day of the year, Yom Kippur, when everyone was in services praying and fasting with bad breath and gurgling stomachs, we could slip out and walk down the street smoking Bel Air Cigarettes and nobody would say a damn word. "Pete, you're such a baby," Steve said. "Everyone is praying. Nobody will catch us. And who else really cares if two guys are walking down the street smoking? Everyone smokes." Being well under smoking age at eleven-years-old did not faze him one bit.

We then broke the Yom Kippur fast by eating slices in a pizza parlor down the street from the synagogue and were kicked out for being eleven and smoking. I was mortified. Steve took it in stride and even told the owner to "go fuck himself."

Steve Goldstein became my idol. He had no fear and was always up for mischief. His fearless leadership brought me a little closer to being Jim Rockford. Jim Rockford wasn't afraid to get caught smoking in someone's backyard and then give the angry adult other kids' names so they notified the wrong parents. Nor was he afraid to steal a couple of beers out of his parents' refrigerator and drink them in his basement while they were right upstairs. And, he certainly wasn't afraid to egg the neighbor's house in broad daylight. Moreover, if the police questioned us for a neighborhood prank, Steve would argue with them and unbelievably hold his own to the cop's complete frustration. I heard once that in school he was suspended because he argued with a teacher that he didn't have to show up for homeroom because it wasn't a valid class. He said you didn't even get a grade for it, so how could it be legitimate?

I wanted to be just like Steve and always tried to emulate him. But he always had more guts and his mind worked in the order of a genius. However, even at eleven he was never happy with life and always seemed to be somewhere else in his head. When we did something wrong, his whole heart and soul was in it. He didn't care what happened, just as long as the window shattered, the egg hit the driver in the convertible or he got away with the carton of cigarettes. He was fearless of consequences, something I wasn't.

My friend Steve ended up dying from a drug overdose in his early thirties. I feel guilty for going off, living my life and not staying in touch with him. After all, I was the one who convinced him to try pot in the first place. I don't think I could have saved him, I just think I could have been a better friend and checked in with him now and then. My guess is that Steve was so intelligent he couldn't stop seeing the irony in life and the pointlessness to human existence. He saw no way out except through drugs. And Steve was the type always to chase the dragon looking for the ultimate high.

Steve loved *The Rockford Files*, too. But he'd spent time in L.A. and saw some of the things I had dreamed of at an earlier age. Apparently it didn't matter to him. He lived life on a deeper level. Steve altered his consciousness because it was the only way he could keep from being overwrought with hopelessness. I think we shared the same depression, just on two different levels. One day he pushed the limits and lost. He always did have more guts than I.

The Feelgood Express

Her Goatliness picked me up in a stripped-down 1981 Oldsmobile Cutlass Ciera, a car she inadvertently used as a battering ram due to her poor driving skills, and took me to Pennsylvania Hospital on an icy cold winter afternoon in 1986. I was a little nervous because I still wasn't exactly clear what I had in common with my mother, so how was I going to be made to feel better? On top of that I wasn't all that sure she was feeling so normal herself.

The hospital itself was only two stories, desolate and institutional-looking. It was off of a main street in West Philadelphia and really set back away from the block. Most entrances to other wings of the building seemed completely closed off to walk-ins. I didn't see nurses running around or hear any "code blues" over the paging system. No wheelchairs, stretchers or gurneys. We were definitely being routed to a specific outpatient wing.

We checked in and sat in a paneled waiting room. I hadn't seen a panel job like this since the early seventies in my friend's rec-room basement. It made me want to play air hockey and drink root beer. And nobody in the waiting room looked at one another. Everybody seemed kind of nervous or had something to hide. As I suspected, I was in a psychiatric hospital outpatient wing.

"Mom, this is the lollipop factory, isn't it?" I used Jim Rockford's name for a mental institution.

29

She looked confused, head cocked to the side. "What are you talking about?"

"A psychiatric hospital."

"Yes, Peter. What were you expecting?"

I guess I should have put it all together sooner. "This. It is just weird to confirm you are seeing a psychiatrist and now I am going to see him, too."

"Dr. Mendelsohn has helped transform my life and I think he can do the same for you. You don't have to be sad anymore these days. There are medications for that."

Medications. "Are pills going to make me never feel sad again?" I asked. I wondered how a pill would make me feel better and what does feeling better feel like? It all seemed so easy. Shouldn't everyone be taking them?

My mother didn't answer. She seemed a little annoyed by the question.

My mother appeared to be the same person to me as always. Have these pills been making her feel better? What does she feel better about? The thing that really made an impression on me was that she was letting me in on her secret. She was admitting to me that she had some sort of psychological problem and had been seeking treatment for it. This must have been a big deal for her, admitting this to me after twenty years. I started thinking back to her sudden disappearances to the hospital for "a rest" when I was a child. Was this where she went? The puzzle was starting to come together. Suddenly I was intensely interested in what I might learn about her, even though this was supposed to be about me.

Dr. Face Melt stuck his pale bald head out of his office door and motioned for us to come in. His name was actually Dr. Meyer Mendelsohn, but he looked like his old sagging face was melting down into his shirt collar with those half glasses sitting on his nose and safety cable around his neck to keep them from melting, too. He had horrible posture as well. Couple that with a monotone cadence to his voice and he was a complete caricature of himself. I thought *he* needed some pills to feel better.

My mother seemed excited to see him and was beaming. They seemed to know each other well. We sat down on the couch. I surmised my mother had probably worn her ass print into his couch. It was a good fit and she snapped right in.

My mother spoke first. "Dr. Mendelsohn, I have been watching Peter ever since he was a child. And he seems to demonstrate a lot of the signs of depression I have. Recently I have noticed it has been especially bad. Do you think what has helped me could help him?"

"Jesus Christ," I thought, "She's been watching me suffer since I was a child and just now she is trying to help? What was she doing before, trying to beat and torture the sadness out of me?"

"Well, that could be, Sally. Studies have shown severe depression to be hereditary. Why don't you leave the room and let Peter and I have a moment alone?" requested Dr. Face Melt.

My mother looked like a little girl who had all her balloons popped at the county fair. She begrudgingly went into the waiting room. I think she felt like she made the diagnosis and it was only fair that she got to follow through on the treatment.

Dr. Face Melt actually wasn't a bad guy to talk to. He asked me a series of questions as if he already knew the answers but wanted to hear it from me without coaching. Was I sad all the time as a child? Did I feel like I couldn't control my emotions? Did I frequently feel hopeless? Did I have trouble concentrating? Did I feel inadequate? Was I especially sad at particular times of the day? Had I felt that way all my life? Did I understand why? For fifteen minutes he asked me exactly what I would have wanted to tell him if I had known to correlate these feelings by understanding that they're related.

Then Dr. Face Melt told me about a medication he would like to prescribe. An antidepressant called Elavil that would make me feel better. I'd take it at bedtime and every other evening I'd raise the dose up to a particular amount. Then I'd come back and see him in a month.

He opened the door to call my mother back in. She practically fell in with a glass stuck on her ear. She immediately snapped herself back into her seat.

"Sally, it's incredible how much he is like you. And since Elavil has worked so well with you, I am prescribing it for Peter." He handed me the prescription. "Doctors are just starting to understand the role heredity plays in psychological make-up." He handed me the prescription.

My mother drove me to the pharmacy and then back to campus, all the time telling me how medication was going to change my life. The problem was I could not fathom how. All I knew was that I was officially severely depressed, enough that I needed to take pills.

Now I was a true mental patient, which was a moniker I did not relish. I was diagnosed with severe depression. Nobody could know. Especially my four roommates. I'd never hear the end of it. My roommate Greg once got so drunk he urinated on me in bed because he thought he was in the bathroom. That had been six months earlier and total strangers on a campus of 40,000 were still saying, "Hey, did you hear about this guy who pissed on his roommate in bed?" One time a girl at a party tried to tell Greg the story not knowing it was he who was the actual pisser! No, nobody could find out.

So I started the Elavil at a very low dose, not knowing what to expect. And to paraphrase Lou Reed, "It hit me like a mother-fucking-son-of-a-gun." I got happy. Things that used to make me sad didn't anymore. The sunlight on Sundays. Walking to classes. Eating in a dining hall. It was like every time my brain wanted to get sad, Elavil stepped in and gave it a lift before it even went there.

And the more I took the better it got. Sometimes for no reason at all I would get this feeling of excitement in my stomach like I was about to go on an all-expense paid cruise of the Mediterranean. Soon I always felt happy. I wanted to be around people. And I wasn't afraid to speak with them. I'd talk to anybody. Moreover, I always seemed to say the right thing and I never second-guessed myself.

The most incredible thing was the improvement in my concentration. I could sit in a class and actually pay attention without effort. Elavil also allowed me to study for hours and not take a million cigarette breaks. As a matter of fact, I actually quit smoking after ten years. I had a newfound contentment that gave me never-before-experienced patience.

I was positively giddy. And when I took my handful of bright orange pills at night, they knocked me right off to sleep. Plus Dr. Face Melt was more than happy to push things to the limit. If Elavil kept making me happy, he'd up the dose. I guess eventually I hit a limit even a buffalo couldn't handle and he capped it out. But I couldn't imagine feeling any better by then and people noticed. Nobody could put their finger on it, but they just saw a change in me. And I saw a change in myself. Sometimes I'd just be sitting alone and I'd realize I had a smile on my face. So I'd break into song about how much I loved Elavil. It wasn't bad. I was going to submit it as a possible advertising jingle for the drug.

However, there were a few side effects that weren't so great. I had constant dry mouth. So much so that my lips would constantly crack and bleed. When it got really bad I'd actually start to lisp from dehydration, making people think I had a speech or hearing impediment and talk very slowly to me. And in the late 1980s people weren't prancing around with bottles of Evian to replenish their fluids. Plus Elavil dried me out so much I think I would have needed to drag around an IV bag to stay hydrated. I could have put it on a pole with wheels for easy transport around campus.

Also there was the weight gain, which I counterbalanced by only eating fruit and salad. And when I veered from my diet, I felt extremely guilty. I was like a girl about food.

But the worst side effect was when I had an ejaculation; I practically had no sensation. Maybe a tiny tingle. And the semen didn't spray out like a healthy fire hydrant, more like a trickle from a rusty faucet. There was nothing manly or pleasurable about it. I was the one guy in the world who could literally fake an orgasm. But I told myself it was a small price to pay for such an amazing life transformation.

Eventually anger set in against my mother. I was furious that she let me suffer for so long and kept everything about her condition secretive until she felt ready to let me in. What I didn't realize was that like a gay person, she was just coming out. And, I was the first person she came out to. I was like a trial balloon. And in later years when everyone climbed onto the psychotropic pill train, I'd get my fill of her talking to me about medications till I was nauseated. Her life became a quest for ecstasy through the miracles of medication and she constantly tried to get me on that same strange, never-ending train ride she was stuck on, the Feelgood Express, with a destination that would never let her "get off."

Hide and Shrink

I'm not exactly sure what's in the Hippocratic Oath doctors take, but I do know it's a little hypocritical. Part of it is "to do no harm." Yet some psychiatrists charge $450 for fifty minutes, $10 a minute if you have to speak with them on the phone in crisis and five dollars for every prescription they have to fill with hefty finance charges if you are a little late paying your bill. And almost none of them bill your insurance directly. Think of it, you have enough problems if you have to see a psychiatrist. Now you're bankrupt, too.

Of course, this is if you can find a psychiatrist. Actually, many of them now call themselves psychopharmacologists and just deal in psychotropic drug treatment. If you want to talk about your problems you need to find someone else. They don't do windows into your soul.

But finding a psychopharmacologist is the real challenge. Here you are feeling like you want to die and you can't find one who is taking new patients or a case as severe as yours. Each time you get snubbed you get another referral who in turn passes you off to someone else and so goes the never-ending cycle. At some point when you finally find a doctor who will see you, you have to wonder what is wrong with them that they have a hole in their schedule. Did one of their patients commit suicide? Then you have to ask yourself, are they really that good in light of this knowledge?

Once you do find a psychiatrist who treats bipolar, they fit into one of three categories. The first category is the doctor who goes by the book *The Physician's Desk Reference*. It's a guide to all medications, what they are used for and dosage instructions. If you get a brand new psychiatrist or one who is afraid of lawsuits, they cling to this thing like it's a life raft. You can burn down their house and they still won't let go. Everything they do is in small conservative moves, never straying too far from the *good book's* recommendations. If the book says Lithium is the first line of defense for bipolar illness, that's what you'll get, even if you've taken it before and it makes you retch. And if you start taking a drug that is making you feel better, get used to not feeling one hundred percent. The *PDR* probably doesn't recommend taking the dose you need to feel your best.

That is like my good ole' Dr. Herman Munster. I actually loved the man. He was my psychiatrist for eleven years in San Francisco and we built a close bond. I call him Dr. Herman Munster because he had a flattish head, walked with his arms slightly out in front of him like a zombie, was tall, very kind and never ever wanted to upset Lily or disappoint little Eddy. He also knew me better than anyone. But when it came to making me more comfortable with the medications I was taking, he rationed them out like gold bullions. It was maddening to know you needed more of something to finally feel better and Dr. Munster didn't want to stray one iota from *The Physician's Desk Reference*, which also recommends bloodlettings for flu-like symptoms.

When I was married to Debra I had numerous overdoses of pills and alcohol where I ended up in the emergency room, and I was in a severely depressed state. However, I became masterful at not having to be 51/50'd, which allows the hospital to hold you for seventy-two hours if they think you are a danger to yourself or anyone else. All you have to do is make sure you don't say you were trying to commit suicide. We both knew me being in the hospital was a waste of time and often made things worse.

After one such emergency room visit while under Dr. Munster's care, it was obvious *The Physician's Desk Reference* was out of ideas and he was beginning to feel my disease was becoming out of his league to treat. He had a psychopharmacologist colleague, Dr. Thomas, who was supposed to be a big deal at the University of California San Francisco Medical Center. Herman reached out to him over and over about evaluating me to no avail. Either Dr. Munster had no respect in the medical community or Dr. Thomas was too full of himself to waddle over and answer the phone.

Finally I got an appointment. I think Dr. Munster hid in the back seat of his car and sprung up when he was going eighty miles per hour on the freeway to beg him to see me. In fear of his life, he agreed.

I couldn't wait to see this new doctor. And, Dr. Thomas turned out to be everything I had hoped. He understood my exact strain of bipolar and put me at ease that he could have me feeling normal again. And like the cowboy of whom I was in search, he drew three new prescriptions from his holster for me and upped the doses of what I was already taking. And I was so excited about seeing the light, I ran right to the pharmacy to start feeling better as soon as possible. Then I was to have a follow up appointment with him a few weeks later.

I took the pills and started to feel somewhat better, like I was on the correct path. I still had some questions and tried to contact this new doctor and found I could never get in touch with him again. Whether it was by phone or email, Dr. Thomas wanted nothing more to do with my case.

I have no idea what kind of deal Herman struck with him, but it was a raw one. Now I was taking five medications and nobody who knew anything about them was monitoring me. I was infuriated a physician would be so irresponsible. Dr. Thomas was playing with my mental stability like he just threw a new set of tires on his wife's Mercedes without mentioning it to her. He probably figured, how could this possibly be the wrong thing to do?

I can hear him now out on a Saturday night with another doctor and his wife discussing my case. "He'll be fine. These are the right meds. He'll get used to them. Hey, pass the lobster sauce over here. When is the Peking duck coming out? I want the fucking duck. It's been over an hour!"

Well, somehow I found a psychopharmacologist who was actually reputable and could *also* take me on as a patient. Even before my first appointment we talked on the phone daily trying to get my medications right so I could start functioning again. He did it without the help of *The Physician's Desk Reference*. He had experience with many different drugs and dosages and wasn't afraid to make bold moves. He honestly cared about how I felt and what I thought.

The doctor was as knowledgeable as he was compassionate. He even had a ponytail but wore it in a very professional manner. For some reason that made me like him even more. I was sure he smoked pot. A ponytail is like a cab with its roof light on. It means it is available for a fare. In the ponytail wearer's case, the person is available to smoke some weed.

So now I was right with my medications. But my doctor felt I still needed to talk with someone on weekly basis. There was a lot going on in my life; I was mainly unhappy in my marriage and this was a major issue.

I decided I wanted a woman for a change. I had been talking to male therapists my whole life and wanted a female's point of view. That's when I met one of the sickest people I have ever had the displeasure of knowing. She was a psychologist who needed to be in a psychiatric hospital in-patient program before she caused any of her patients to kill themselves and possibly take her with them. I later learned one of her patients actually had committed suicide right before I started seeing her.

She was a short, bespectacled, whiney Jewish lesbian in her early fifties. The minute I walked in her office she opened up all the windows, turned on a fan and started "honking" like she was clearing her sinuses. Apparently she could not tolerate cologne and the next time I came to see her I was instructed not to wear any.

So the next time I went to see her I went cologne free. However, she angrily accused me of wearing cologne and opened the windows and brought out the fan again. I finally got her to believe me that I was not wearing any cologne. So she decided it was the dry cleaning fluid the cleaners used on my suits. Next I was forbidden from wearing clean suits to my appointments.

Then there was the therapy itself: we spent most of each session, after she sniffed me and was sure I didn't deliberately bring in any pleasant odors, talking about her own problems and medications. It was ridiculous. I felt like I could not get a word in. And she never made suggestions when we talked about me, she literally told me what to do. After several months I wanted to dump a bottle of Dolce & Gabbana cologne over my head and walk into her office with all my fresh dry cleaning and see if I could make her end up in the hospital.

Instead I left her a phone message that I was discontinuing therapy. She called me back and got me right away. The conversation went something like this:

"You can't leave therapy. You have a lot of issues. Leaving is running away," she said.

"You have a lot of issues. I feel like my sessions are all about you. No hard feelings. This just isn't working."

The doctor's whiney pitch started to rise. "How can you say that? As a professional I never talk about my personal life unless it specifically relates to something we are discussing."

Let's see, I knew all about her lover, their arguments, her medications, her health problems and her own psychosis which in no way relates to me. I wanted to get her the fuck off the phone. "Whatever. Look, you have too many idiosyncrasies, too. Cologne, dry cleaning fluid, etc. It's too much trouble to keep seeing you. You're neurotic. I need a normal doctor."

She started squealing. "I can't believe you are saying such things. You need to come to your next appointment and..."

"Sorry doctor. Take care and good luck." I disconnected my cell phone while I could still hear her high-pitched voice scorching the earpiece. I was worried she had burned out the wires in my phone or something.

Thankfully, I did find a great female psychologist who doesn't seem to have a problem with dry cleaning fluid or working out *her* issues in my therapy session. She cares about me and I can feel it. One time when I was in an inebriated and pill-laden crisis, she actually came to my apartment with her partner in practice and sat talking with me for three hours instead of calling 911, bringing the evening to a safe conclusion. I don't think they teach you this in shrink school. And, she charges on a sliding scale if need be. Sometimes I want to touch her to make sure she is real.

I have heard other psychiatry horror stories as well. Friends whose doctors will only see them once a month, and do not return phone calls in the interim. Doctors who will not take you off a medication in spite of the fact it's making your mental state worse. And my favorite, doctors who don't take the time to listen and hear what you are telling them about how you feel. How you feel is the whole point of treatment!

The medical profession is overrun with these turds and, when you are not in your best frame of mind, you are forced to weed them out and find an honorable psychiatrist or therapist. Hopefully you have a sane friend or significant other who can help you navigate through the ego-maniacs and those enjoying their final days of their medical license to help you get the treatment you deserve. Doing it on your own can make you insane. Or, I should say, *more* insane.

Urbane and Insane

To me one of the most annoying things to see is a semi-fat girl with dark circles under her eyes, multiple face and ear piercings and pink Kmart cotton panties slovenly sticking out of her jeans, drudging through a job at Starbucks which she loathes. She is also living with a roommate whose boyfriend she can't stand, in an apartment building where she is at constant war with the landlord and a downstairs neighbor forever banging on the ceiling screaming at her to turn down the Pink Floyd. And in between bong hits she croaks, "I wouldn't be such a mess if I didn't have such a fucked up family." Meet Bipolar Girl.

I have little tolerance for people who blame everything that has gone wrong with their lives on bad parents or a rough childhood. There are a lot of people in this world who have had a raw deal on the home front but grew up to be successful functioning adults. And, they never used their tough upbringing as an excuse.

Don't get me wrong, nothing is more annoying than when a parent or grandparent gives you the cliché, "We walked to school in the snow with newspapers tied around our feet because our parents needed to read our shoes. But we made do." You have to stop and think about some of these stories and say, "Right on. You did do that. I don't think I could."

Take my Grandfather Sam, my mother's father. His parents came to the United States from Russia and were both dead by the time he was

41

fourteen, making him an orphan with nowhere to go. So he lived with various relatives sleeping in their vestibules, went on the road selling magazines when the relatives closed their houses down for summer vacation, put himself through college and then started a successful circular distribution business with his best friend.

In those days newspapers did not do inserts, so an alcoholic in a uniform delivered advertising to your door. It allowed my grandfather to get married, buy a house, have 2.1 children and live a middleclass life. And with all life's ups and downs, not one single time did he blame a problem on a rough upbringing. He blamed the blacks for crime, democrats for the country going to hell, wouldn't trust a Chinaman and would never buy anything from a gentile that could be bought from a Jew. However, he never blamed his upbringing, even when newspapers killed his business in the mid-seventies and his thieving business partner stole all his clients and went to the competitor.

In fact, he bragged about how he made it on his own. He was proud that adversity taught him to be stronger. Sam Seidman was one guy you'd never see taking a bong hit and moaning that everything bad happened to him because he had a fucked up family. And there are millions of people out there who don't blame their families for all their adversity, either. You just don't hear about them because they don't complain.

So, you are not going to hear me blame my family for the bad things that have happened to me in my life. I am telling you my story, but my actions have put me at the point I am today. Nobody banished me to San Francisco. It was my choice to move 3,000 miles away from Philadelphia and live my own life.

It's not that I don't think my family was insane. They were actually urbane about it – never wanting anyone in the world to know they popped a cork and always trying to look their best in public. But behind closed doors they were a mess. Aside from my mother and maternal grandmother, I'm not sure if any other family members were actually bipolar. However, their sanity was definitely in question.

Take my paternal grandfather Irv, who even in his seventies was a very attractive man. But oh, how he hated his suits and hangers. One time when I was visiting him in suburban Washington D.C., he waged war on his suits. He had a huge mirrored closet in his bedroom spanning an entire wall, filled with neatly hung color-coded suits of all styles. One day he came home from work and was undressing as I sat on his bed. He was telling me dirty jokes and all the slang names he made up for female genitalia. As he hung up his suit pants they slid off the hanger and took down another soldier with them. Enraged, he tore down two more comrades and gave them a full dressing down with language that would have made an American soldier in Vietnam during the late sixties in a monsoon-drenched mud hole taking direct fire turn red. Nobody hated those suits, slacks and hangers more than my Grandpop Irv. And eventually, after a couple of swigs of Old Grandad and a True mentholated cigarette, he was fine again. But I think his wardrobe was a bit shaken.

It was the same thing if you changed the seat setting on his Sandstone Yellow Lincoln Mark V. After cursing and yelling at me that it would never be the same again, he'd get over it. To see this handsome, well-manicured and distinguished gentleman in his seventies, you'd never know the insanity that arose if an inanimate object disrespected him.

But when he wasn't lambasting his wardrobe or calibrating the seat settings in the Lincoln, he was one of the most influential people in my life. He always spoke his mind and gave me the confidence to come out of the closet as an atheist. He was also the only person who truly "got me."

Once when I was thirteen and visiting him with my dad and his girl-friend, my father started teasing me to impress her. Normally I didn't pay too much attention. He meant no harm. But, I hated this woman he was dating with a passion. She emulated the character Julia Roberts played in *Pretty Woman,* only in real life. She'd pretend to have been deprived and abused by a mean Hungarian husband and was not used to being treated like a human being. So, everybody would go out of their way to make her feel comfortable and took delight in giving her the very best of everything while she looked on with her big doe eyes. Plying her with top shelf liquor, taking her to the fanciest restaurants and posh lit-tle getaways, all just to witness the amazed expression on her formerly impoverished face. The little bitch never had it so good. In return, she was totally subservient to my father. He was in foot rub city. However, I always saw through her fake "Eliza Doolittle" smile. And the rain in Spain fell mainly on the guy she was milking for all he was worth, which happened to be my dad. Eventually, when she was done with him, she ran off with one of his clients who was apparently better off than he. It was just awful.

My grandfather saw the dismay on my face and took me into his home office to have a smoke together. He'd tell me my dad was in love and I should ignore his girlfriend. However, my father was very critical of me. It was obvious I was not following the most conservative life plan. But my grandfather wanted me to follow my own path in life, not my father's conservative blueprint. Unfortunately, my grandfather ended up a watch salesman and not an actor or doctor like *he* would have preferred. For me, he wanted what I wanted: to take some chances and be my own man.

He taught me about being courageous. So when I was fourteen and visiting him in Maryland, he made me drive his new Cadillac Fleetwood Coupe DeVille through heavy downtown Washington D.C. traffic to suburban Maryland. I had never driven a car before, although I'd been dying to get behind the wheel since I was a little kid.

Before we pulled out of our parallel parking spot I asked, what if I crash? My grandfather said he hated the Cadillac and wanted another Lincoln. Then he put his foot on top of mine, which was already on the accelerator, and pushed it down hard. We went squealing into traffic like a Cadillac cannonball. I had a blast. And of course my father lambasted my grandfather when he found out about what we did. At fourteen I could already sense me driving a car was going to be one more battle I'd have to fight with my father. Insurance, gas, maybe a car... It all cost money.

My father loved my grandfather, but never really saw the greatness in him. He just saw an overly-indulgent heavy drinker. I wish I had more time with my Grandpop Irv. He died when I was a freshman in college. It was in those later years I really could have used him.

The only thing that confused me about him was that he really liked my dad's girlfriend. I thought if anyone could see through her he could. But she was a flirt and definitely turned on the charm with him, especially since he was always the bartender. And all guys fall under some kind of weird spell when a decent looking woman starts flirting with them. Personally, I know anything with a vagina that shows an interest in me makes me want to be extra friendly.

My maternal grandfather was also funny, but it wasn't on purpose. He always drove a Cadillac and thought anyone who didn't live in a big city was a hick. He used to refer to my father in Bethlehem as a "small town Democrat." He saw himself as urbane and completely evolved.

But Mr. Evolved would always lose his Cadillac every time we went to a Phillies Game. You could count on it. He'd take me to a night game in spite of the fact that I didn't like baseball. I couldn't see what was going in the field so he'd spend the evening trying to explain the game, which to me was like hearing him read me the instruction manual to a 747. Then we'd head for the car at the end of the eighth inning to beat the crowd. And like clockwork, he couldn't find the green '73 Caddy. We'd walk around for an hour. He'd ask people if they'd seen his green DeVille, only one of probably 1,000 in the lot.

Eventually he'd start to lose his voice and screech, "I can't understand it!" Then he'd decide it was stolen. He'd call my grandmother who was already nervously sitting in the bay window waiting for us to come home. "Edna, it's Sam." He could barely speak. "I'm with Peter at Vet Stadium. The car was stolen!"

By then she was chain smoking Parliaments in her housedress and started calling the relatives giving them the news. She'd begin with my mother. "Sally, Sam and Peter are at the Phillies game. His car was stolen and they're alone in South Philly."

My Pop would finally tackle a security guard and tell him the whole story, delivering a sputum shower in the progress. The guard would be disinterested and suggest he wait until the lot emptied out before he called the Philadelphia PD. And sure enough, the lot would empty out and there would be Pop's Green DeVille.

This is how my grandfather lived his life. Panic first, think the worst and later learn he'd acted like a spaz for no reason. Only, he never seemed embarrassed that he'd gone overboard. In fact, I don't think he noticed. He'd spend the whole next day telling the story like he was almost proud of it. He had absolutely no control over his impulses and could not evaluate his own actions, even in retrospect. In his mind he was a great entertainer with his stories. He felt right at home at Bookbinders, a classic old Philadelphia restaurant and celebrity hangout that, like my grandfather, is now gone but thought of fondly in many people's memories.

Also, my grandfather Sam had to be one of the best all-time grandfathers in the world. He doted on his grandchildren, my friends loved him and he really had a spectacular life, in spite of the fact he couldn't afford to keep up with the Finklestiens. But he put on a great show with a live-in maid in a small house and a neighborhood that screamed "Chevrolet."

My maternal grandmother was a *confirmed sighting*. My mother told me she had seen a psychiatrist for years and took some sort of psychiatric medication. It was obvious she had some deep-seated issues. But nobody ever talked about it. Of course they all talked about me, but never about her.

The insane behavior I noticed most in my grandmother was her anger. She was always the most loving grandmother to me, but I think she had a list in her head of people she thought had wronged her or a family member. Bring up one of those names and she'd let loose a verbal rampage shrouded in a cloud of Parliament smoke. Sometimes you could barely see her through the cigarette smoke and only hear her venomous raspy voice somewhere in the middle of it. She sounded like Froggy on *The Little Rascals*. Of course first she'd close all the windows, so none of the neighbors could hear.

And when she got going she couldn't stop. "And do you know what he did to me in 1962?". She would then dig out some minor incident about a person and equate it to Pearl Harbor. On and on with the same story and details for hours while we sat in a booth at Hymie's Deli as she nursed down an enormous center-cut tongue sandwich and coffee. She always ordered the same thing and I couldn't believe my Nana could eat that much. She'd even consume all the condiments on the table while she continued her diatribe.

And my grandmother's five brothers often treated their only sister like an afterthought. Yet to her, they were next to God. One of them was actually named Phoenix. He was the greatest gynecologist that ever wielded a speculum. She couldn't mention his name without throwing in that he once was Chief of Obstetrics at *Albert Einstein Hospital* in Philadelphia. And of course every place she had ever gone, done or experienced was "the finest." Even her friends were "the finest." Her proctologist was "the finest." I often wondered who made that determination. Was there some AAA Guide that told you where to find "the finest" of everything? How were these things rated?

But my grandmother Edna was always good to me. And she adored her grandchildren and great-grandchildren like it was a sickness. She would stare at a picture of my daughter Madeline for hours and study every inch of her face. Sometimes when I'd send her a new picture she'd call me on the phone because she detected the slightest bit of redness around her lower lip and was concerned. She also told great stories about the old days and how mean her father from the old country was. The man was a bully. Today he'd be in jail for child abuse. Was he "the finest," I often wondered?

We'd often sit in the kitchen, drink horrible instant coffee, smoke cigarettes and talk for hours. She was the only one with the patience to teach me to drive when I turned sixteen. She also loved a good drink at the bar before dinner. When I moved to California we talked every Sunday for at least half an hour in the afternoon like clockwork for seventeen years until she died. On Sundays I still sometimes think, "Don't forget to call Nana."

Then there was my paternal grandmother, Jean. She wore so much make-up under a five-layer blonde hairdo I was amazed she could hold her head up. She also wore very colorful expensive clothing and big semi-precious stone rings and fine jewelry. People would stare at her wherever she went and she loved the attention. She lived in Bethlehem so she stuck out like a fur coat at the supermarket. And she was very loud about everything she did. Her laugh was combustive. When she walked into a room everyone knew it. She was Queen of Bethlehem, Pennsylvania. And Bethlehem was her paradise. Nothing else mattered. She lived in a completely different reality. She came to Bethlehem from Philadelphia in the late 1940s.

Did I mention she could fart the label off a bottle off Manischewitz? Not only that, but she took pride in it. "Did you hear that one, baby? Your grandmother can still knock one out." She was hilarious. I don't think she could help herself so she just went with it.

But I admired my Grandmother as a tower of strength. She had been married three times. She'd withstood two divorces and her third husband, the love of her life, died of cancer. She herself survived cancer and several heart attacks. In her late seventies she lived alone but, incredibly, still dated. Plus, she was an amazing cook. And I always knew she loved me.

However, my grandmother's solution for everything was Bethlehem, Pennsylvania. No girlfriend? "The most beautiful girls in the world live in Bethlehem!" Looking at colleges? "Stay right here in Bethlehem and go to Lehigh like your father. Then you can be a lawyer with him in Bethlehem." Moving to San Francisco? "Why the hell would you want to do that baby? Bethlehem has everything San Francisco has!"

I also know that she suffered from some deep depression, especially in her younger years. While helping clean out her apartment after she died, my father found a lot of her writing and some photos of herself signed, "Jean, Sadness Herself." And I've heard on several occasions she dealt with a lot of psychological-depression related issues.

My father also believes that Bethlehem is the center of the sophisticated world. And he delights in proving to people it has everything Philadelphia does, the city of his birth.

In fact, my father is Bethlehem's staunchest cheerleader. I remember when Bethlehem got their first Starbucks. He practically put me in a wheelbarrow and pushed me over there he was so excited. And he doesn't even drink coffee. He just wanted me to see what a big deal Bethlehem was becoming. Moreover, when he gets started on the Bethlehem restaurant scene I have to hear about all the world-class restaurants that have come to town. "Just as good as in New York or Philadelphia," he crows. However, the ones I have been to look nice but the food is very T.G.I. Friday's. I keep looking for the curly fries every time we go into one of these brass-adorned happy shacks.

He also is devoted to his wife, Mary. A very nice-looking and intelligent woman in her early sixties, my father is obsessed with keeping her looking in her early forties. And, through exercise and a minor surgery here and there, he's done a superb job. Moreover, with all my dad's idiosyncrasies he requires someone who can handle his plethora of needs. Mary truly "gets him" and makes it seem easy. Obviously he makes her happy as well. It's a good marriage.

One idiosyncrasy is my father's self-imposed health issues. He has a standing weekly appointment with his internist and was the first person to my knowledge to practically help the surgeon install his own pacemaker. He actually requested one like he was picking out a new cell phone. I think he saved some money because his has a rotary dial and receiver protruding from his chest. He can't calibrate it over the phone like the new pacemakers, but he can call the doctor on it to make an appointment. However, he does get a lot of annoying sales calls.

I do feel sorry for him because he should be enjoying the good life in his retirement, but instead he is literally consumed with worry and fear that my brother or I will screw up our lives. It makes him extremely anxious taking on the burdens of our divorces, ex-wives and business trials and tribulations.

As I've hinted at before, my dad has a weird relationship with money. Not only does he like to spend it judiciously, but also wants my brother and me to do the same. He was a bankruptcy lawyer, so I guess it goes with the territory. Consequently, I try not to talk about finances with him. He's never lived on the edge, so I think it scares him when he gets a glimpse of the wanton risks I have taken. Whenever he comes out to San Francisco to visit and I'm driving a different car or have two at a time, he looks like he is literally going to be sick. Keeping a car until the wheels fall off or the technology on it becomes embarrassingly out of date is more his M.O.

Consequently, I don't think my father is a bipolar sufferer. I think it's more an anxiety of the unknown as he gets older. I may have inherited his insanity about getting in and out of the car properly, but I don't think he's bipolar or unipolar. And I agree, there is a proper way to get in and out of my car. It's important to keep it looking new without scuffmarks on the insides of the doors from passengers with sloppy foot control.

So yes, my family was and is insane, but at the same time trying to be urbane. It's a funny combination that has brought much amusement to my brother and me over the years. And instead of complaining, I've decided to let it be entertaining. Otherwise I think I'd have to drive off a cliff.

The Boy Down the Street

One of the bipolar "sprinkles on top" I've been blessed with is obsessive-compulsive disorder. It's actually quite common. For many people it shows up in the form of "checking" or "counting." I have both.

The best example of checking is not being able to leave the house without checking, double-checking, triple-checking, and so on, that the stove is off. The first time I look at it I can tell it's off. But for some reason I don't trust my evaluation. Or I think something caused it to turn itself on when I wasn't looking. So I check again. And again and again and again. It's maddening and I can't stop. And I don't want anyone to see me doing it. I know it is irrational but I still can't help myself. Even when I think I'm done after countless checks and am finally on my way to work, I begin to doubt myself, turn around and drive home and check the stove again. The whole time I know it's ridiculous but it just can't be tempered. What if I'm wrong and the apartment building burns down because I left the stove on? Sometimes it takes until midday until the urge to keep checking the stove becomes dulled enough with other thoughts to stop torturing me.

And it's often not just one thing. Another obsession is if I go over a severe bump in the road while driving my car, I spend the evening running in and out of the parking garage climbing underneath my car examining the undercarriage for damage. I don't even know what I am looking for, but I just have to repeatedly examine it. And if I do actually get a scratch on my car, I ruminate on it for hours from all vantage points. I try to minimalize it in my mind. I try rubbing it until the paint comes off and it looks even worse. I get into such a frenzy that a one-inch key scratch in my mind makes my pristine vehicle look like a broken-down jalopy. The first call in the morning I make will be about trading it in or scheduling extensive bodywork. Moreover, until the repair is made or I sell the car, that scratch is never off my mind.

A third example of my uncontrollable compulsions is that I can't go to sleep at night until I make sure I take my medication twenty times over. If you think it can drive your roommate or significant other crazy, imagine what it does to you. You're sane and rational, yet you have this ridiculous compulsion you cannot control. In and out of bed for an hour checking your medicine cabinet and counting pills. It's maddening and there is not a damn thing you can do to make yourself stop. Because if you do make yourself stop, you lie awake all night worrying about it. Are you going to feel bad in the morning? If you missed taking your pills what kind of day are you going to have tomorrow? Will you be sleepy and sluggish or all amped up? Concentrate. Concentrate. Shit, you'd better go check again.

I had a friend in high school that had the compulsion sickness as well, although in 1983 we didn't exactly know what it was. I just knew he was like me with the checking. I once saw him pull out of my townhouse parking lot, stop and then get in and out of his car examining the situation under the driver's seat for almost an hour. God knows what he thought was under there. A possible short-circuited wire that could erupt into a fire? I could think of a million reasons he might have been checking. It was funny watching him for a while. I even yelled out the window, "Hey Willy, power seat riding up your crotch?"

He just gave me a confused look and mumbled, "Uh, yeah. It's this thing." I immediately felt bad because I knew what he was going through. But he knew I was a fellow OCD sufferer and me teasing him was my way of saying, "This compulsive shit sucks."

At least to my knowledge bipolar disorder was either not discovered or formally identified. And I'm sure the plethora of correlating symptoms had not been associated with the disease. So, when people were obsessive-compulsive nobody handed them a mood stabilizer or antidepressant with an anti-obsessive-compulsive acting agent that mutes the urge to a degree.

As a kid I was an obsessive-compulsive superstar. I had to say my prayers at night at least ten times until I thought they were perfect enough for God to accept them. If I was watching a TV rerun, I had to say, "I saw this before," twenty-five times in a row with perfect pronunciation before I could watch it. When relatives were around I had to tell each one how much I loved them at least twice or I was afraid I'd hurt their feelings and they'd go home and die that evening. I had the weight of the world riding on my shoulders. I always thought I was one missed "I love you" away from killing my grandparents.

And, if my bladder was ever the least bit full I had to go pee immediately so it would be completely empty. I was always afraid I'd have to go badly during an unexpected car trip, or if the plumbing broke, or the bathroom suddenly became occupied or something was to happen where I could not relieve myself, I'd panic. Consequently, I always wanted to make sure the tank was empty. Whenever the opportunity arose I was compulsive about taking a piss.

Being that I was a nervous, highly emotional child you'd think my mother would have asked, "Peter, why are you so nervous and running to the bathroom all the time? Does your penis hurt or are you just worried about something and it's making you go a lot?"

Instead my mother went down the street to the neighbor's. Some kid had the opening of his penis enlarged because he wasn't getting enough urine out when he went to the bathroom, so it caused him to go a little more frequently. God knows how, but my mother heard this and wanted to find out more. I can imagine her knocking on the door asking the kid's mother to discuss her son's penis.

Half an hour later she ran back up the street, took a look at my penis, decided the opening was too small and scheduled an appointment for me with an urologist. She tells me they are going to widen the hole of my penis so I could get more pee out and wouldn't have to go to the bathroom as much. Mind you, this was before the doctor had even examined me. I became hysterical about the prospect of someone taking a tool to my tool.

The next day I went to school and everything was fine in the morning. Or at least as fine as it could be if you were going to have someone cut into your penis with a knife. I kept picturing my penis with a big gaping hole like Ronald McDonald's mouth, only vertical.

In the afternoon after recess my second grade teacher took me aside. She was very pretty and even at eight-years-old I wanted to be cool in front of her.

"Your mother told me about your operation," she said with a comforting smile. "I think you are very brave. Until then anytime you need to use the bathroom, you don't need to ask. Just go."

I wanted to die. My mother had gotten the embarrassing word to my teacher within twenty-four hours of her self-diagnosis. But this was not as bad as when our gym teacher took me to the far end of the locker room that day and wanted to know what was going on with my genitals. I had to tell GI Joe, who probably circumcised his own seven-incher at a frat party on a dare, that I had a small penis hole that needs to be made bigger so I don't pee all of the time. He was very understanding but I knew he'd be telling the story at some bar that night laughing his ass off with his gym teacher buddies.

I knew this operation wasn't the right thing to do, but I couldn't explain why. I didn't understand obsessive-compulsive behavior. I'm not sure anybody in 1974 had that much of a handle on it.

I don't remember the doctor's visit where my mother most likely hammered the small-penis-hole diagnosis out of the urologist, but I do remember the operation. The doctor was actually a distant relative and very compassionate. I think he felt sorry for me for being my mother's son. I wonder if he really thought this was necessary, like a plastic surgeon that is asked to make someone with Dolly Parton-sized breasts even bigger.

Was he thinking, "Aw, what the hell. It can't hurt"? Or, "Sally is a lunatic. I'll make a tiny incision on her kid's pecker and get her off my back. If there is a problem, I'll blame it on the moil in '66 who did the circumcision a few days after he was born."

On a side note, if Jews are supposed to be so smart, why do we let some old guy with a knife that's had a little too much Manishewitz into our homes to slice our baby boy's penises? And as our children are screaming in pain and bleeding we all celebrate? It's absolutely primitive. While we are at it, why don't we have the moil slice off that boil on grandma's nose? Oh no, that needs to be done by a doctor in his office. But a home circumcision by a drunken hack on a newborn is perfectly okay? I don't get it.

So I remember lying naked and cold on the hard operating table like a plucked chicken getting ready to have vegetables shoved up its ass and then dropped into a boiling pot of water to make soup. The nurses, probably in their twenties, were really nice and tried to calm me down when I freaked out that I wasn't asleep yet and not to start cutting. Then I felt the needle in my arm, literally saw a checkered flag go down and was whisked away to slumber and slicement.

I woke up groggy in a crowded recovery room with my penis stinging like crazy under a piece of gauze. That's when I decided I was never going to look at my mutilated organ or go to the bathroom for the rest of my life. But the time came for me to get up and go into the men's room with the doctor. He wanted me to pee. I think the entire hospital heard me go. I had stitches, it was bloody and when I went it felt like my insides were coming out of me. In a very *small* way I can imagine what women must go through with childbirth. And with every bright red squirt of bloody urine I resented my mother for doing this to me out of what I think was boredom. When I finally did look down I almost gagged at the bloody crisscross stitching. It made me wonder if this was what Frankenstein's penis looked like.

To this day I have problems from this unnecessary procedure that I think slightly disfigured me. No matter how hard I shake after I urinate, a little seeps out when I put it away and I have to stand under the electric hand dryer in the men's room to dry off. And if there is no dryer, I have to wave paper towels in front of my crotch to air dry. Plus, I always have been self-conscious as to whether my penis opening is a little bigger than it should be. And, I'm positive it's caused me to get several urinary tract infections.

But worst of all, I have never been able to shoot straight. My penis is a wildcard. I have accidentally shot guys standing next to me in public urinals and almost gotten my head broken open. Every time I go pee I don't know if I'm going to hit a wall, the floor or an innocent bystander. Sometimes I even shoot down my own leg.

But as much grief and embarrassment as this has caused me, blaming my mother isn't going to change anything. She treated a psychological issue as a physical symptom. But in 1974 nobody had the right information. So this is what happened to people. Epileptics had lobotomies. Depressed people had shock treatment. And little boys who wanted to make sure their bladders were empty had their penises sliced open by mothers who had nothing better to do.

Matter Over Mind

I had been in the psycho ward once before in college. Dr. Face Melt took me off Elavil because of the side effects. Apparently there were newer antidepressants he wanted me to try. Elavil was a very old drug that took a sledgehammer to your brain. These new drugs just zeroed in on the depression and left everything else alone, causing fewer side effects.

But the new drug I was on had not been working for months and I was at the point where I wanted to die. I was rolling around on the floor like a beached whale, unable to find any kind of physical or mental comfort. My mind felt like it was going to explode if something wasn't done to calm it. The depression was like somebody had put a wet blanket over my head and it was incredibly uncomfortable, annoying and impossible to think of anything else except about how badly I wanted it off.

I was living with my girlfriend, Jacqui, in the Art Museum Area of Philadelphia and had taken a few extra pills to help myself sleep, half hoping they'd kill me. I was so depressed that she had panicked and taken me to the emergency room the previous two nights in the wee hours of the morning and they said there was nothing they could do for me. I sat there and begged for someone to do something for me. I tried to explain how I felt. I told them I was on antidepressants and Dr. Face Melt was out of the country. I had nobody to call.

On the second night, they gave me something to help me sleep and then brushed me off. I was a nuisance compared to their gunshot wounds and knifings that seemed to keep the emergency room jumping. I don't think they realized my mind was planning its own murder.

So the next night I ingested the entire bottle of sleeping pills they gave me, half hoping to die and half hoping to bring it to someone's attention that I was suffering. It seemed a little ironic, but you have to be near death to get help. Nobody is interested in a prediction. But I wanted to go to the hospital. I thought the doctors would make me feel better. It just took the entire day to get me admitted because my dad drove my half-conscious and limp body to every hospital in Philadelphia until he found one that would admit me as an indigent and his insurance company would not have to be involved in the matter.

My dad rushed into the city when Jacqui called to say how bad off I was. They both decided I needed to get to an emergency room. My dad was truly concerned but he didn't want to pay anything for my care. "God-fucking-damn it, I'm getting nickeled and dimed to death. It never fucking stops. Do you know how much it cost to get new tires on the car? Let the hospital sue you when you get out. You have nothing. They'll drop the whole thing." Jacqui was with us and couldn't believe what she was hearing. We drove around for what seemed like hours, shopping for a hospital that would take me.

So I spent a week in an inner city hospital psycho ward admitted as an indigent. My first night was in the basement "dry out" unit because they had no beds open. I laid awake all night listening to a heroin addict go through withdrawal symptoms. Between the moaning and throwing up I was getting the shakes myself. I heard every chunk of vomit hit the floor. Soon it became liquid and sounded like a fire hose. Then it was just dry heaves. I felt horrible for the guy. Withdrawal is exactly how they say it is, and nothing but a thin curtain divided us so I heard every cry of pain and plea for death—but nobody seemed to care. Everyone else was dealing with his or her own dementia or deep in a drug-induced sleep. There was one orderly for the whole unit and he seemed more concerned about when someone would bring down his dinner than the heroin addict bringing up his.

The next day they finally had a bed for me. I ended up spending a week sitting around in a mental ward getting blood tests, watching TV and smoking cigarettes in the company of a wide assortment of people with various mental illnesses. The TV part was hard because there was one man they'd always roll into the day room strapped to his bed. Every few minutes he'd scream out, "I just want to die! Somebody please kill me!" It would scare the hell out of me and make watching television seem completely insignificant with this guy suffering only a few feet away. I knew how he felt. Amazingly, none of the other patients seemed to be fazed. They actually appeared somewhat annoyed. After a while in the psych ward, things that would make you stop in your tracks and stare on the street barely make you turn your head.

And all my medical team seemed to be doing was trying a new antidepressant on me and waiting until it started working. Every now and then they'd tweak the dose, but I had no psychological counseling. It was all chemical to them. I was an organism that needed to be metaphysically re-balanced. How I felt during the process was of little consequence.

I was lonely. I tried to find someone in the ward to connect with, but everyone seemed to be completely out to lunch. I once started a conversation with a girl who seemed to be my age. She was relatively cute with blonde hair and blue eyes. I asked her what part of Philly she lived in and we were making small talk. I got up to get a cigarette out of my room and when I came back into the hallway the orderlies were dragging her away as she was screaming like a wild woman. I watched as they restrained her on her bed and stuck her with a needle, to her extreme protest. I asked if she was okay and someone kicked the door shut. I never saw her again. I was rattled.

Then there was Mr. Norton. He was an elderly black man who looked just like the guy who played the garbage man on *Chico and the Man*, a TV show from the mid-seventies. I could tell at one time he was very tall, powerful and in charge. Now he was completely bald, limping along but still with a real attitude. I could barely understand him when he spoke because it was a combination of slang and mumbling, but everything that came out of his mouth was a joke about staff, a patient or the ward in general. And all he wanted to do was laugh. He'd hide semi-conscious patients in wheel chairs in rooms where nobody could find them, throw pieces of toast at one patient during breakfast causing him to pitch hysterical temper tantrums, insist on wearing diapers so orderlies would have the objectionable task of constantly changing him, tell the hard-ass nurses how ugly they were "Fred Sanford- style," and just induce general chaos in the ward.

Personally I think Mr. Norton was completely sane and someone warehoused him there. He was doing his best to be disruptive. The longer they thought he was crazy, the longer he got to stay there. The next stop was probably a state hospital or an old age home. My guess is he did not want either of these places; I didn't blame the old guy.

I spent a lot of time just sitting with Mr. Norton. I loved being around the class clown. Sometimes I'd almost forget my predicament and how bad I felt. But one night I was depressed about my whole situation: the inappropriateness of being stuck in a place where they even watched you sleep and go to the bathroom, not having any talk therapy, having my medication not work and knowing I only had my low-paying job to go back to. I just wanted to lie in bed and stare at the ceiling. Next thing I knew, around 11:00 P.M., Mr. Norton was standing over me in the dark, illuminated only by the glow of the light from the hallway. I was shocked to see him. He just started laughing. I didn't know what was funny, but it made me laugh. Just seeing him standing over me with his bald head, big brown bug eyes and gaping grin with bad bridgework was entertaining. And the harder I laughed the harder he laughed. Eventually we were wailing. I think tears were running down my face.

Orderlies and nurses came running into my room. Patients were waking up and wandering in with even stupider looks on their faces than they already had. The "just let me die" guy started screaming his mantra. And amidst it all Mr. Norton was dragged out of my room still cackling and I was told to be quiet and go to sleep. But my body still convulsed with silent fits of laughter. I just kept picturing the old guy standing over me stirring up the shit. I think he was trying to send me some sort of message. Maybe something as simple as, "Just keep laughing no matter how depressing things get."

I never did see Mr. Norton again. The next day they let me leave and he was nowhere to be found. I didn't ask because I didn't want to know.

All I knew was I didn't belong in an inner city psycho ward. I convinced the doctors the medication was working and agreed to seek outpatient therapy through their outpatient clinic.

I was even more depressed after the hospital stay than before. The prescribed lithium was barely working. I hated my job. Jacqui and I were not getting along and I was sleeping in a separate room. Neither of us could afford to move. Unable to deal with my illness, she started seeing other guys and had sex with one once while I was home. I have never been so deeply hurt in my life, but we both wanted the apartment for ourselves and hoped the other would move out. Plus I was stuck going to therapy with this psychiatric medical student once a week who was just plain mean to me.

The wet-behind-his-ears Dr. Conrad and I spent our sessions having him criticize me for the fact my ex-girlfriend was fucking a guy in the next room bothered me, I wasn't making enough money at work to pay him his full rate and for being naïve enough to believe that medication was going to be able to help me significantly. I tried to tell him how the Elavil had once changed my life, but he told me, "That was then and this is now."

Dr. Conrad was a total runny-nosed elitist and if I met him in a bar I'd be making fun of him in his argyle sweaters and perfectly creased slacks. He had no idea every time I walked into his office for a weekly visit that I'd just spent fifty plus hours a week trying to sell airtime on a classical music radio station and was worn out and frustrated. I was a brand-spanking-new sales person: twenty-two-years-old, unpolished, unconfident and panicked about making my goals and paying my bills while I was wrapped in a thick cloud of depression. Everything and anything that anybody said to me in the workplace was analyzed over and over again in my mind until it meant the worst possible thing and then shoved itself into my psyche like a dagger to break me down. And now I had to deal with this Sigmund Freud wannabe.

Finally, enough was enough. I found out about a doctor that was willing to help me through a family friend. So I told Dr. Conrad to go fuck himself. He proceeded to call me several times a day telling me how sick I was and that I needed to come back. He even got hysterical on the phone and screamed at me that I couldn't keep running away from my life like this. But I wasn't running away. I was going to see a real doctor, not a medical student with the bedside manner of a hemorrhoid. My guess was that my defection was going to get him a really bad grade and he'd have to explain to everyone how he came to have a patient who hated him. It must have been devastating for a young medical student. Personally, I hope it made him decide to become a podiatrist. I don't think you can be condescending to feet.

The new doctor was perfect. He was not an alarmist. He listened to me and showed great compassion. I told him how I loved Elavil and maybe a little lower dose would eliminate some of the side effects. He agreed. Finally somebody was listening to me!

The best part was it worked almost immediately. I was suddenly my old self again. I was back in the game and I owed the world to him. I was confident, happy and excited about life. Jacqui had moved out of the apartment, I had a new girlfriend and started making commissions at work. Life was good. It felt good to be alive. Whenever I thought of my new doctor I almost got a tear in my eye. Why couldn't they have done this for me in the hospital? Why did I waste six months being tortured by sniveling Dr. Conrad? All I kept thinking was, "Baby, I'm back."

Eventually even Jacqui wanted me back. We started seeing each other again, which was consistent with our break up and make up pattern that had been going on for years. My sales team even went on a cruise to the Bahamas. I had also made enough money to buy a decent lineup of double-breasted suits, matching silk hankies and tassel loafers. I strutted around Philadelphia making sales calls dressed like a mafia boss. I wasn't worried about anything except keeping my shoes shined. Then I got the California bug.

Go West, Young Man

Getting back together with Jacqui was like putting on a comfortable old shoe. We fought a lot, but also knew each other better than anyone. And I was attracted to her in every way. I even loved the smell of the air coming out of her nostrils. The fighting was almost routine.

Plus, I loved her parents and they loved me. Her elderly father was a dermatologist who reveled in maintaining a pauper's image by wearing tattered clothing and driving old cars. His office was in a poor white section of Philadelphia, and he'd let patients work on his car as payment. Every time I'd see his grey 1977 Chevy Caprice it had drill marks all over it that resembled bullet holes, newspaper on the seats so you wouldn't sit in the tar used to mend the ripped vinyl and a steering wheel from a random Buick that didn't even match the color of the car. What could have possibly been wrong with the steering wheel that it needed to be replaced? Jacqui's dad didn't think to ask.

He also loved to eat like a slob (sometimes directly from the plate without the use of utensils), drink whiskey out of medicine bottles, smoke cigars, watch PBS in his boxer shorts and fart every time Jacqui entered the room. This last practice truly embarrassed her. And he seemed to do it on purpose, which made me feel sorry for her. However, he was one of the most educated and compassionate men I had ever met. I loved smoking cigars and drinking whiskey with him while listening to him speak of philosophy. He was a good man. He probably should have been born in the 1800s. He was a total history buff. And he treated me like a son. I also think he couldn't believe there was actually a young man who could handle his daughter's demanding temperament.

Jacqui had anger, and a lot of it was against him. And if I were a girl growing up in a house where my dad farted in front of my friends, I might be angry too. At the time I just sloughed it off because I was having such a good time with him and all guys love hearing a robust-sounding fart. I think I should have tried harder to see it from Jacqui's point of view.

Jacqui's mother was a simple woman. She was the peacemaker. All of the fights between her daughter and I could be settled with a veal chop. I loved her veal chops. She loved me like a son and I loved her as the mother I always wished I had. She listened to my problems and always tried to make everything right. She knew Jacqui and I loved each other. She also knew we fought, but she felt our love would prevail and that I would always take care of her. Unfortunately, with my mental illness Jacqui did not want to take care of me, whether I needed it or not. And I can't blame her for that. Nobody should have to do that unless it's his or her own choice.

Before she saw me fall apart and end up in the hospital, we kept breaking up and getting back together again because we did love each other, even though I loved her parents and wanted to be around them, as well. If we had just been friends and not lovers we would not have fought so much. But sex ruins everything. And she needed a lot of it, and thanks to Elavil, even when I could get it up, ejaculating had the thrill of taking a leak.

I remember when Jacqui decided she wanted me to be "her first." We decided to rent a hotel room on Roosevelt Boulevard in Northeast Philadelphia to consummate. We had the music, the wine, the lighting – and then I noticed *Dirty Harry* was the Friday night movie on channel ten. As much as I wanted to make love to her, I secretly wanted to lie there with a beer watching *Dirty Harry*. On the sex-dulling drug Elavil, Clint Eastwood had more appeal to me than having sex with a virgin. I put the man who carried the big .44 caliber handgun out of my mind and focused on my own pistol, praying it wouldn't disappoint. I wanted this to be nice for Jacqui.

What non-mentally ill people who do not take psychotropic medication don't realize is that we give up so much to stay sane. You wanna feel good? Great, but you will not be able to enjoy orgasms, you'll be forever constipated, have blurred vision, your mouth will always be dry and you'll gain twenty pounds. A lot of people opt out of the medication because the side effects are more depressing than not being on medication at all. Nothing is for free with mental illness. I don't think people understand this. There is always a price to pay for feeling good, or at least not suicidal.

When I started doing better in business and was less depressed, I decided to take a vacation. I chose to go to San Francisco and then drive down the coast to Los Angeles. I had been west when I was twelve and really liked it. I also decided to set up some interviews with radio stations in San Francisco while I was out there. I was sick of selling ad time for the same old classical music radio station in Philadelphia and wanted to do something dramatic with my life. In Philadelphia my mother was too close for my liking and I was becoming more and more responsible for my aging grandparents. I wanted to do something with my life before I regretted playing it safe. And I told myself these were just interviews. It wasn't like I had job offers and someone was thinking of hiring me. So, I was pretty relaxed about the whole thing,

I took Jacqui out to the west coast with me. Thank god she wasn't enthralled by the mystique of San Francisco. She said the weather was too cold in the summer, the Haight-Ashbury section was too grungy and the people in the city were strange. It was too different from Philadelphia. No row houses, high-rise apartment buildings or shopping malls. I loved it—the 1960s heritage, the rock and roll history, the landscape, the fog, the free-spirited people.

I went on lots of interviews. Most of the jobs I would have taken. The only one I didn't want was one out on the island of Alameda. It was a long ride from the city, the radio station had poor ratings and I could scream louder than their FM signal would carry. How could I sell for a station nobody can hear?

So we left San Francisco, drove down the coast and did the L.A. thing. That was more fun for Jacqui and we did all the touristy trappings. However, California just wasn't her bag. Everything was too new and way out there. It was more like a spectacle. I liked L.A. and thought that could be a back-up domicile should things not work out for me in San Francisco.

When we returned to Philadelphia, I received a phone call. It was from the station with the weak signal, low ratings and pain-in-the-ass commute from San Francisco. They needed a sales rep like me. I knew it was a stupid move, but it solved a lot of problems. It would get me away from this break-up-get-back-together cycle that never seemed to end with Jacqui. I wouldn't be the major caretaker of my grandparents who, as they grew older, were consuming more and more of my time. I'd get away from my mother's insanity, and I'd get to do something adventurous with my life. I figured if I didn't at least try, I'd regret it forever. And I loved California. Not everyone had the stomach for such a dramatic life change. I felt like I was going to throw myself into the blender.

Yes, I'd miss my dad. And I knew he couldn't understand why I was "doing this to him." But just because he never did anything quite so adventurous with his life didn't mean I shouldn't. However, in another sense I think he enjoyed living vicariously through me. And I think my brother was happy for me and looked forward to visiting. He has always been supportive of anything I wanted to do. His opinion is and always was the only one that ever mattered in my life.

The one aspect of my big move that had my family worried was my mental health. Could someone with my condition do this on his own? What if I had a mental breakdown in the middle of nowhere? Who would help me? What would happen to me? Would I end up in the Alabama Home for the Criminally Insane with Billy Bob Thornton talking about "how much them taters cost?" I wasn't going to let "what ifs" stop me. Fuck my brain chemistry. I decided it had ruined too many things for me. I wasn't going to let it ruin this. This six-day trip across the United States in my 1990 Volkswagen Jetta, filled to the brim with clothes and my road bike strapped to the back, was going to be me laughing in the face of the odds and saying a big "screw you" to my mental illness. This was change to the greatest extent. I sang the theme to the Mary Tyler

Moore Show for 3,000 miles. I only wished I'd had a hat to throw up in the air.

The trip was incredible. I saw the entire middle of the country. I met college girls in Lincoln, Nebraska who had never seen an ocean. I had lunch with truckers at Philips 66 truck stops. I saw a horse standing in the middle of the road in Iowa bringing traffic to a standstill, and nobody seemed to mind. I had lunch on the time zone in Colorado and couldn't figure out if it was 11:00 A.M. or 12:00 P.M. I heard crop reports on the radio and stayed in a town in Montana with only one of everything. Someone even shot a .22 caliber bullet through my windshield in the middle of nowhere Wyoming causing me to almost drive off the road. I even went running past the big Mormon Tabernacle Church in Utah and considered taking a leak in their bushes. And, I won $250 in Reno and almost had a hooker come to my room.

I rolled into San Francisco on September 9th at high noon and pulled up in front of my friend's apartment on Post Street, where I was planning on staying for a while. We'd grown up together and were planning on living together. Unfortunately, he was in the process of being evicted and most of his possessions were out on the street. It turned out the phone calls telling me how well he was doing were a bit of an embellishment. He had no job, no money and was getting kicked out on his ass from a studio apartment that I'd been told was a two bedroom. And it was in the Tenderloin, a seedy neighborhood known for its drunks, drug addicts, hookers and criminals.

I felt like I was having a mental breakdown. I wanted to scream for my doctor, my dad or anyone who would listen. But I was 3,000 miles away and alone. I told myself I had to work this out. So I paid off the landlord for a week, moved our stuff back inside and we looked for a larger apartment. My friend assured me he had a job lined up.

I was really putting my psyche to the test. So far, so good. I was actually impressed with myself. I was dealing with my situation and not freaking out. I wasn't crying and gassing up to go home.

So we found a one bedroom. And unbeknownst to me, my friend found my checkbook and paid his half of the rent with it. Needless to say when I found out, he was out of there and I was alone in San Francisco. I had him put in the mental ward of the University California

San Francisco Medical Center. It was obvious his brain had a short circuit. That's what I told the admitting nurse the evening I brought him in. And he was so scared I was going to kill him he nodded his head in agreement. To my amazement they accepted him. I think he said he was suicidal or something. I wish I could get rid of more people I don't like that easily.

I ended up moving into a studio apartment in the same building, went to my new low-paying job and started my new life in a new city on a new coast not knowing a soul. And I wasn't sad, I wasn't giving up and I was even more determined that I was going to make this work. Still only diagnosed with severe depression, I took my medication and refused to let my handicap determine how far I could go in life. Although every day was a struggle I was super proud that I was struggling 3,000 away from my comfort zone. I had a lot of friends who were not afflicted tell me they didn't have the guts to make a move like this.

It took a really long time until I felt like I had a life. I inadvertently got involved with a gay running group on Saturday mornings, which did nothing for my social life. I thought I was just running with a bunch of guys in my apartment building and a few of their friends, then realized everyone in the group was gay. But I was lonely so I figured they could at least be friends. A lot of us went out to breakfast afterwards and it was fun hearing all their conversations. The problem was I started getting invited to dinner parties and other activities. There were also a couple of guys that had latched on to me. So I thought the right thing to do was to make sure they knew I was straight. But there is a weird thing about gay guys – they tend not to believe you. They think you are playing hard to get or you have not fully come out of the closet.

One guy called me on the phone after I repeatedly turned him down on a date and was furious at me for being gay and not knowing it. I soon learned straight guys and gay guys couldn't truly be good friends. The realization made me a little sad. I found them very interesting as individuals and although they might feel the same way about me, if my genitals weren't part of the package, they lost interest fast.

I had to divorce myself from the group. But there were a couple of guys in it I really missed. It struck me as very unfair that we couldn't be friends because sexuality was so important to them. You can be platonic with girls but gay men seem to have a hard time being platonic with straight guys if you spend too much time with them. They all want to accidentally kiss you, pat your ass or sneak a peek at what a gay friend described as his favorite part of the male anatomy, "the basket," or the penis and testicles in their underwear resting pouch. I was at a gay dinner party when I heard about the basket. Broccoli came out of my nose. I never even heard a girl speak of it before. Years later when I told my ex-wife, she laughed the hardest I'd ever seen her laugh at anything.

Among other things, I also had sex with a black girl who called me on the phone and said she saw me on her TV and wanted to marry me. We talked on the phone for a month before I agreed to the first meeting. Her story was ridiculous, but she knew so much about me down to my exact physical description. So one night we met for sushi and she was an absolute African Queen. Braided hair, drop-dead body, dressed-to-kill miniskirt and amazing almond shaped eyes. Best of all, she insisted on paying for dinner. To this day I cannot uncover the real reason she sought me out.

So eventually I slept with her. Then she disappeared and her vitamin salesman boyfriend called to let me know she was schizophrenic, had disappeared and asked if I could help him look for her. I spent an afternoon with Bob trying to track her down. He was so frail and sickly-looking it appeared as if he needed the vitamins instead of selling them.

We learned from a youth hostel she stayed at that she had gone to work on a whaling ship headed for Alaska. After that Bob kind of got attached to me and mourned her constantly. It was all he talked about. Then he got weird and wanted to discuss how great having sex with her was with someone who had experienced it, too. The thought of me having put my penis in the same place he had put his scared the living hell out of me. I stopped answering the phone or the door when he stopped by. I had to hide out for a month until he gave up on hanging out with me. I couldn't even look at my penis for weeks because it made me think of withering little Bob in his tattered army jacket and crooked plastic glasses in a sense having touched genitals with me. I was disgusted with myself. It didn't matter that I wore a condom.

My best friend was a short, bald, sixty-two-year-old man I worked with who had a thick Boston accent. He wanted to go to singles bars with me every weekend and try to meet women. But our ages were so vastly different it was impossible to find two girls out together with a similar age span. And nobody wanted to hear him incessantly banter about how much he hated his ex-wife. However, Jim loved my depraved sense of humor and was happy to be the butt of my jokes, as he had nothing better to do. So he latched on to me and became my sidekick, ruining my fun almost everywhere I took him. And whenever he got near a girl I liked, he'd either flirt with her himself, pressure her into finding him a friend or find another unique way to piss her off and ruin things for me. But I liked him anyway and always told myself he was a good friend and that when the chips were down he would be there. And the truth was, I think he felt like the "cool uncle" to me and that made him feel like he had a purpose.

Finally I had a year-long relationship with a real Jewish career girl who had wild curly red hair, was way to full of herself, and insisted on telling people she was from Chicago when she was actually from a tiny little town in Indiana. Believing she was from Chicago, I found myself going back with her to meet her parents and spent a hot and humid August week in Munster, Indiana. Didn't she think I'd realize we weren't in Chicago when I saw the cornfields?

I also hated the fact that her name was Debbie but she insisted on spelling it Debe. She did it to be less generic, but nobody could ever pronounce it properly. And, if they found out she spelled it that way of her own volition, they'd just plain get annoyed.

Back in Indiana, her dad was a little henpecked and obsessed with barbequing, but a decent man. But her yenta mother with the tight pants on the fat body, oversized hanging shirt, diamond rings and big silver hoop earrings was another story. She was just like Debe, only fatter. All nouveau riche and full of herself with a condo done in 1980s style glitz. And the two of them were so loud together. It's one thing to be without class, but to purposely call attention to it just doesn't make sense to me. The two of them had to be at the center of everything. Everything they did and had was "da best." At one point her mom took her out shopping and later told me she dropped a deuce on her daughter. She meant she just spent $2,000 on her in a clothing store. I took it into the realm of bathroom humor, telling her not to tell anyone and maybe nobody would notice.

We finally did go to Chicago where Debe had literally scheduled meetings with friends down to the hour. One guy she took shopping for furniture, another she counseled on a relationship. It was like the city of Chicago was waiting for her visit so she could help everyone furnish their apartments and sort out their lives.

Things were no better with her in San Francisco. She was always calling me at night right before TV Land's nightly airing of *Dragnet* was about to start and I'd miss it and *The Beverly Hillbillies,* too. Plus she'd send me on errands, like to pick up her laundry, only she couldn't remember which Chinese cleaners it was at, so I'd have to hopscotch all over the Mission District looking for her panties.

The worst part about her was that she always wanted to be in the middle of controversy and other people's hardships. Consequently she made sure everyone knew she might be bisexual. This way she could be at the vortex of the straight or bisexual world and get noticed for her unusual orientation. But even her own gay sister saw through it and called bullshit on that.

She visited and did shopping for gay men who were dying of AIDS. Although I think she really did care about them, I believe she loved being part of the grieving process with their families. She ate up all the attention when the families and friends would thank her for providing so much comfort.

But I was so afraid of being alone and didn't have the guts to break it off. I didn't want to go back to how I felt when I first came to town and my phone never rang, in spite of the fact that I wasn't miserable. And then one night when I dropped her off at her apartment after a night out she very kindly broke it off. I tried to be somber as I said goodbye and pledged to still be friends, but I peeled off down the road cranking "Pictures of Matchstick Man" at full volume, playing the dashboard drums. I never felt so free in my entire life. I was laughing out loud and people in the cars next to me were staring at me at traffic lights. They could hear my delirium through my open sunroof. I got home just in time for *Dragnet.* I broke open a beer and danced all around my studio knowing nobody was going to come between me and Jack Webb's 1968 Plymouth Coronet police cruiser that evening. I relished the phone not ringing.

After all this madness with the stolen checks, schizophrenics, homosexual running groups and vitamin salesmen, I met my future wife, Debra. My coworker at the Classical radio station had a Passover Seder for her Jewish transplanted friends in San Francisco. Debra was her upstairs neighbor invited down for the dinner. I thought she was absolutely lovely and we spent the evening enjoying each other's company. I was a little unsure she would like me because she had an MBA, surmised she made much more money than I and came from a more sheltered life. However, the next day at work my coworker put her phone number on my desk and said Debra would like it if I called. I was thrilled.

Debra was normal and suddenly my life became the same. We associated with normal people. We did more normal things. We had normal aspirations. People weren't seeing me on their televisions. I wasn't hanging around with Bob. I was done with the gay running group. Life was finally *as I thought* it should be. At least, at that point in time.

Jonesboro

All my life I have been obsessed with acquiring material possessions. Not just anything, but things I have decided I need to complete my persona. And when I fixate on something I have to have, I enter the state of Jonesboro.

Jonesboro is a fucked up state without laws and common tenets of decency. When you're in Jonesboro, if you want something you'll shape reality until it makes sense and justifies buying anything that your little heart desires.

When I was young, Jonesboro was just a fantasy. I remember being eight-years-old and loving the Lincoln Mark IV my grandfather drove. But I knew I was eight years away from even getting a driver's license. Moreover, I knew my father was not going to buy me one and I surely couldn't afford one when I turned sixteen. So I spent my nights lying in bed fantasizing what it would be like if I were suddenly gifted a 1974 Lincoln Mark IV with Opera Windows, overstuffed velour upholstery and moon roof along with a provisional driver's license allowing me to drive at eight. Oh, what a time I would have wearing my velvet sport coat, silk shirt and cravat cruising all my friends around as I received secret missions from the U.S. Government to follow up on as an undercover agent.

Never happened. I knew it never would. Even if it could at that time my father would never permit me to have any fun while he was so miserable with my mother. My father never was a big proponent of people having fun. It's too decadent. To this day I'm afraid to tell him when I do something that is really exciting.

But then I got older and along with that came a job, a little cash, some credit cards and a credit rating. And all of a sudden when I started jonesing for things, I realized I could get in the game. Suddenly I could get the Omega Planet Ocean wristwatch with the orange bezel, the Mustang Shelby GT 500, the $1,500 David Yurman rings, bracelets and necklaces. And once you get used to living in Jonesboro, you spend a lot of time jonesing for the next big purchase, whether you can afford it or not. You can't have just one expensive Swiss watch. After all, you can't wear a diver with French cuffs. And when everyone is wearing French cuffs, you're going to need the jade cufflinks, not the fabric ones that come with the shirt. And a haircut for under $50 is going to make you feel like you went to the supermarket and had it done in the checkout line. In Jonesboro, good is good. And if you don't have it, you feel like shit about yourself.

The problem is, living in Jonesboro isn't cheap. And the reason you're in that state is probably because you're obsessive-compulsive. It also means you probably can't afford to be there. So sooner or later you are going to get in trouble in Jonesboro. But you'll keep on jonesing all the same. You can't control it.

Most people don't understand the compulsion. It's just like the "checking compulsion" or the "jinxing compulsion." If you don't update yourself to the latest styles, something will go wrong. You'll jinx yourself back to a time when you were at your un-coolest. When you wore corduroy pants and Dennis the Menace shirts to school with a Timex. You won't be able to compete in today's world as an equal because you won't have the right armor. You'll be a loser and everyone will see it. You won't have the self-confidence you need to go out into the world and set it on fire. You'll constantly be looking at yourself, comparing yourself to others and feeling like you're not good enough. Once you've been to Jonesboro, you have to fork it over. You have to pay to play.

I've been to Jonesboro many times. Jonesboro has caused me to buy cars I can't afford, to make "step down" purchases of expensive rings and bracelets after I just bought a $4,000 watch because I needed the right accessories, to buy thousand-dollar suits because they fit me "so right," to buy classic cars as misguided investments and to rent apartments in exclusive neighborhoods I have no business living in. But at the time I *had* to have these things. I couldn't imagine living without them. There was a rationale for every decision I made. But when it came to paying the bills, Jonesboro was a pretty expensive state to be in.

Credit agencies and lawyers harangue people for letting their lives get this out of control. But I don't think they understand that for some people, it's beyond their control. And you'll liquidate your savings account, 401K and your kid's college fund before you'll sell that Tag Heuer Carrera watch you're sporting on your wrist or the 1973 Cadillac Eldorado Convertible you drive on weekends that makes you fancy yourself a "collector."

Obviously if Jonesboro is cleaning you out financially, you've got to get out. You have to realize that you don't need material objects to the extent that you think you do. That nobody even notices if you wear the same watch every day, only have five suits or haven't spent top dollar on a haircut. But if you're obsessive-compulsive, it's a tall task. Because when you feel you look good, you project confidence. And if you've had a life of depression, worry and not feeling as good as anybody else, it's a pretty good feeling. So I need to make the argument that sometimes it's worth it to risk it all and stay in that state. Is it the healthy solution a good psychiatrist would recommend? No, they'd say it was a form of self-medication.

So many of us bipolars with obsessive-compulsive disorder have mortgaged our future and embraced life in the great state of Jonesboro to feel confident and good about ourselves. To always be excited about a next new purchase. To artificially stimulate ourselves without medication. My favorite thing is to fixate on a purchase on Monday and get so worked up about it by Friday that I'm the first one in the store Saturday morning to buy it. I become monomaniacal about it. Then I spend the weekend transfixed on it. And by Monday I'm over it and have set my sites on my next item of lust. It's the cycle that I've come to live by.

So I've been broke in Jonestown and I've been riding high. But I don't see myself leaving. Not unless I suddenly develop bad taste and an infatuation for Ross Stores. It's an embarrassing state to be in. I often try and hide my purchases or belittle their importance and value. But when you get a new car every year it becomes a little embarrassing, especially in a bad economy. However, not getting one is sheer misery. Jonesing is a very uncomfortable feeling. Nowadays you can take a pill for it. The problem is you lose interest in everything. Nothing excites you. Life is just a bodily function. It's like walking to the mailbox. Sometimes you don't even bother getting dressed. I don't know about you, but I'd rather be jonesing. At least you feel something.

Married to the Mob

The biggest mistake and best thing I ever did in my life was to get married in 1995. The mistake was that I married the wrong person for the wrong reason and had in-laws that made feel me like "the guy who married our daughter and now we have to be nice to him." The good part is that now I savor being single like a sailor just pulled out of the ocean after being on a life raft for ten days, having already starting drinking saltwater, hallucinating and snacking on a crewmember.

My ex-wife Debra knew I suffered from severe depression and that I took a truckload of Elavil to stay out of the dark hole. She was a good person who loved me and was very highly educated. She went to Cornell for undergraduate and graduate school. And she lived in France and Belgium for two years. But she didn't have a lot of life experience. While I was thirteen, running around Philadelphia smoking, getting high, ditching school and hanging out with a thirty-five-year-old divorced neighbor in her apartment watching her get drunk until she passed out on her bed, she was out playing spin the bottle in a gorge in Upstate New York.

Yes, I was paling around with a thirty-five-year-old neighbor at thirteen with a key to her apartment. In retrospect I think, "What was wrong with this woman? She could have been arrested for getting me drunk, high and allowing me to skip school." But to a thirteen-year-old mind "she was the only one who understood me and treated me like an adult."

After my escapades with her were uncovered by my middle school vice principal, her apartment quickly went vacant. I couldn't understand where she went and why she didn't say "goodbye." I did hear from another neighbor that she had moved to Florida. "What a bitch she turned out to be. Leaving me in the lurch like that. Where would I go to smoke?"

Back to Debra. She completely idolized her family and dreamt of me being very close with them; unfortunately, that never happened. They were not inherently bad people. Instead they just were very caught up in their own lives and related to each other by talking about how well they were doing in their respective business ventures. One time I was at dinner with Debra, her brother and divorced father as they practically all stood up at the table and started trading resumes.

I found her brother the most annoying. He was basically a nice guy. But he measured his success by how many countries he'd been to and lived in. He actually did start a business in Russia that was pretty successful when it was quite dangerous to be in that country. Now he is spending the rest of his life trying to recreate that adventure, hop-skipping around the world.

However, all he ever talked about was his life abroad. And subconsciously he'd developed this strange accent I called a "world accent." It sounded a little English, but mostly how female starlets spoke in the movies back in the 1940s. Very proper annunciation with a little flit at the end of each word. And of course it would lead many people to inquire where he was from, and then it was off to the races. He had permission talk of his travels in all his glory.

Since his family fancied him a good speaker, he asked if he could make a speech during our wedding, which meant a lot to my ex-wife so I acquiesced. But it turned out to be about him and how he just flew in from Russia. I'll never forget that, especially since he actually had the speech framed and gave it to us for a wedding present!

I did care a great deal for my father-in-law. He was a 350-pounder with one of those beards that looked like it was carved with a stylus knife. It did not follow a natural looking hairline. And everyone was always concerned about his weight and smoking, too. To his credit, he was always concerned about everyone in the family. And if something was wrong, he always flew in and took control.

Big Papa liked to be in control of everything. And because he thought I was taking his daughter away from him and his influence over her, he didn't like me very much. One time early in our relationship he was visiting us in San Francisco from Boston and we were going to lunch. He suddenly grabbed Debra, put her in his rental car and told me to follow them in my own. It happened so fast I was still standing on the sidewalk ingesting the instructions when they were gone. Maybe his instincts about me were right?

And as long as I knew him he would ask me a question but never wait for the answer. He'd just start talking right over me. I think he wanted to be polite by showing interest in me but then his impulsive nature to talk about himself got the best of him, he realized he really didn't care and went on to the next thing before I could even get two words out.

Debra was constantly trying to find ways to get Big Papa and me closer. I suggested having him teach me to meditate—a practice he was very much involved in and had been doing for several years. So one afternoon in a Radisson Hotel room in Burlingame California, right in the flight path of the big jets at San Francisco International Airport, he set up his alter, candles and assorted paraphernalia and we knelt before it. It was there he spoke foreign words, waved around some smoke, gave me a mantra and I was in. Then we meditated together.

I never tried so hard *not* to feel anything, which is exactly what I was supposed to do. I tried for months to not feel anything. Big Papa and I discussed my progress routinely. I hung in there for a few months because finally I felt like I was getting closer with him, but eventually I decided my, by then properly diagnosed, bipolar mind could not shut itself off and would never be able to meditate. Big Papa and I didn't talk much about it after that. Acquiring a taste for Indian food was the only thing I ever got out of it.

Big Papa had remarried a woman from Texas. She was actually very proactive in reaching out to me. I honestly did like her. She meant well. It's just that she was from Texas.

It was a crazy mismatch. She was one hundred percent small town Texas and a graduate of Winnebago University with a major in Above Ground Pools. So she did her Texan routine while Big Papa was an educated Northeasterner doing his intellectual thing, making them an amusing duo.

Debra's mom was sweet but we never connected. She didn't have a mean bone in her body, but we had absolutely nothing to talk about. I dreaded being alone with her. You could hear a pin drop. She didn't even let out a sigh with a "yes, yes, yes" now and then. Nothing. And I'm not sure it bothered her. I always wondered what she was thinking. Maybe she was meditating.

When together, mother and daughter would just sit there and laugh hysterically. And they had an identical laugh. Plus, I don't think they were laughing at anything in particular. It was just self-combustive laughter. Somehow it would start and the next thing you knew it sounded like two old cars trying to turn over without much luck.

Then there was my mother-in-law's husband, almost ten years her junior. The thing I liked best about him was his passion for strong coffee. We both connected over that. But for an author/psychologist, he had his own issues. Told he had a mild-form of diabetes, he constantly monitored his body's intake and weight, depriving himself of desserts, breads, red meat, dairy, sugar – basically any food that makes life worth living. When we would go out to eat he'd just sit there gaunt and sickly-looking as he painfully deprived himself of all that is good. He did not even drink. He spent most of his time locked in his home office working. Either that or looking at pictures of ribs and corn bread on the internet and jerking off.

Going to their house in upstate New York was so boring. Once you got there you were a prisoner. You were snowed in with nothing to do while Debra and her mother had their laughing fits. And all you got to eat were rations. Not only were her cooking skills lacking, but my mother-in-law was one of those people who just made enough for each person to have one small serving. There was nothing for seconds. You just ate your rations and didn't complain. It was like being on a submarine.

Soon you just learned to do your time in the big house. Stay out of the office with the doctor's computer. Watch a little TV in the day room. Read your bible and keep your mind busy. Maybe build a model airplane or something. Just do your time, don't let your time do you.

The next family member was, as they say in the mob about an associate, "a friend of mine." I really liked my sister-in-law. She was a little wild when she was younger but then she married a nice guy, had three kids and turned out to be a really responsible person who was still a lot of fun to be with. But since she didn't have a resume to trade at family gatherings, she decided to convert to Christianity. And everybody was going to have it shoved down his or her throats at her wedding.

Nobody was happy, especially me. It meant I had to fly to upstate New York, feel like an outcast among Debra's relatives and sit through a boring ceremony. I could care less about religion as I always felt it was a big sham. She could join Satan for all I cared. The one thing that bothered me was that her grandmother would have to see this, and she grew up during World War II. She lived through the atrocities of what happened to the Jews at the hands of Hitler. I felt they should have kept this conversion to Christianity from her. She didn't have to know. It was a sign of disrespect. But every time someone in that family had to fart, they wanted the entire brood to be there to smell it.

Last member of the mob of significance in my life was Big Papa's brother, who was considerably thinner. He was a doctor from Boston and the only person in the family who actually showed an interest in me. This is not to say he couldn't talk for hours on end, but he also listened. And when he did talk it was usually interesting.

And I've never seen somebody so happy to have non-Hodgkin lymphoma in my entire life. Of course he hated the disease, but he loved the treatment. He enrolled in an experimental treatment program at Stanford University Hospital in Palo Alto and sometimes found himself in California weekly for it. He enjoyed staying at our house, playing tennis outdoors in the winter and getting together with West Coast friends. The treatment was going well and he was almost giddy at times.

One September day in 2001 I remember he called me early in the morning as I was staring at the television while I got dressed. Cheery as always, he wanted to let me know he was coming out soon and was asking me about the weather and if I could do something trivial before his arrival.

I couldn't think because smoke was coming out of one of the World Trade Center towers. I wasn't sure what was going on and I was trying to hear the newscaster. So Uncle went on and on and I just told him I'd take care of whatever he needed.

Then I watched a passenger jetliner fly right into the second World Trade Center tower and it exploded into a fireball. As I said goodbye he said to a very stunned me, "By the way, do you see what's going on right now on TV?" It was an afterthought. He meant no harm. He wasn't unfeeling. He just needed to secure a tennis court in San Francisco and then he could watch our country be attacked by terrorists.

Kind of like how I was an afterthought at a family reunion when they took a big picture of the entire clan and did not realize I was still standing on the grass waiting for instructions on where to stand. Nobody noticed I was left out, not even Debra.

No amount of medication could ease how bad that one hurt. That was the moment that I officially gave up trying to fit in with my in-laws. It was about seven years into the marriage and I knew it would never be. In all actuality, I didn't want to be related to these people. They made me doubt myself. Maybe I was not worth wanting to get to know? Maybe they didn't want someone like me ruining their family?

And when they weren't swapping resumes they were playing "Six Degrees of New York Jews." It's like "Six Degrees of Kevin Bacon," only with this game you try to show through six connections that you are basically a New York Jew. Giving people you meet the impression that you have "New York experience" and stereotypical Jewish heritage is very important to them.

Debra and family once took my daughter to Ellis Island to show her the exact spot where her great-grandfather stood when he immigrated to this country. I later explained to Madeline that is where everyone's relatives stood when they got off the boat in the early 1900s.

The funny thing was Debra and my in-laws were not even Bar or Bat Mitzvahed. My ex-wife said she and her siblings never even went to services as kids. There were no eight-hour Passover pre-dinner prayer sessions or break-the-fast dinners to celebrate the end of Yom Kippur. I understood why they were so anxious to be identified as the ultimate New York Jews: because they thought it was hip to be a Jew. They loved imitating the accent of ancient Jewish New York relatives. But to know practically nothing about the religion or to have never suffered many of its tortures, I felt they weren't entitled to the distinction. They were reconstructing personal history. Not that I deserve an award for sitting mindlessly during the marathon prayer sessions forced upon me as a youth, but you should at least have some emotional scarring around the high holidays before you start with the stale Jewish humor.

Debra was constantly making plans to visit her family or have them come to us. This meant I was continuously finding ways to avoid them. I hated the feeling of being an outcast, especially in what was supposed to be my family, too. I wanted someone to make me a veal chop and someone to watch PBS in his boxers with me while we smoked cigars.

And nobody ever reached out to me. No one made it a point to say, "Hey Peter, I've never been in a real radio station. Do you think you could give me a little tour of where you work when we come in for a visit?" No, it was more like, "Hey, when I come in I have some really exciting news to share about this new firm that is interested in my work."

So when I tried to commit suicide a second time it was while married to Debra for a relatively short period and I was new at having in-laws. I ended up in the psych ward at UC San Francisco and was for the first time diagnosed as bipolar. I felt even more uncomfortable around my ex-wife's family. Their thoughts were validated; I was damaged goods. I was now confirmed mentally ill. I had to be treated differently. And I resented it. Bipolar doesn't make you retarded. It doesn't take away your ability to think normally, feel and react appropriately. You just have to always monitor yourself and make sure you're in check with the tenor of each situation. Saying a bipolar can't think normally because of their mental-emotional state is like saying that when someone is crying you have to consider them incompetent of making any decisions for the duration of their tears.

Yeah, I was married to the mob. A mob of in-laws that drove me crazy with a constant fixation on their own self-importance. Debra was very attached to her family. And when I married her I got the entire familia. This is one of the things that ultimately broke us up. Unless you marry an orphan or Bipolar Girl, when you marry a girl you marry her family.

72-hour Hold

It was 1995. As long as Debra's family wasn't around, we were doing okay. But the antidepressant, although changed back to Elavil at a higher dose, wasn't cutting the mustard again. Doctors have a fancy term for when medications suddenly stop working. It's called "pooping-out." I'm up. I'm down. I'm suicidal. I left work early one day and decided I couldn't take it anymore and wanted to die. The depression was unbearable. I just couldn't see a light at the end of the tunnel. I was fidgety and uncomfortable in my body. I felt like I wanted to crawl out of it. Everything I looked at was grey and depressing. I had nothing to look forward to and I was deathly tired of the same old thing. I was just plain old, weary and out of gas. And I felt like nobody was hearing my cries of pain, neither my psychiatrist nor my wife.

I came home midday to an empty apartment, put on The Doors's "Soft Parade" and started taking tranquilizers, washing them down with whiskey as I chain smoked cigarettes, something I hadn't done in years. I just couldn't take it anymore. Work, life, everything was just too much for me. I wanted to escape permanently. The only thing that made me excited was the thought of death.

The more I drank the more courage I had to take more tranquilizers. The music was very loud and I knew it was attracting some attention from the neighbors. But I couldn't stop. The pills and alcohol made me feel better than I had in a long time. So I danced around and sang for a period of time, for how long I can't even guess. My inhibitions were quickly drifting away.

Eventually Debra came home and saw the condition I was in. She could not get me to stop. I was cradling my bottle of whiskey like a baby. And every few minutes I'd take another pill. I was way over the safe limit and mixing them with alcohol made it worse. I could barely walk and was stumbling all over the apartment. She was scared out of her mind and called my psychiatrist. I remember her handing the phone to me and I was yelling something at him. Apparently he told her to call 911.

I kept drinking, taking pills and smoking. I felt like I was floating and having fits of laughter. Next thing I knew the San Francisco Police appeared in my living room along with some EMTs. I was out of my head. They got me to put the bottle down, let me smoke another cigarette and then grabbed my arms and helped me walk to a stretcher in an ambulance headed for the University of California San Francisco Medical Center where I had dumped off my roommate years earlier after stealing my checks. I wasn't sure what was going to happen. I figured I'd dry out and come home. But I had never taken Psych Ward 101 before. I completely sabotaged myself. I didn't know about the 72-hour hold.

Next thing you know I was in the emergency room and a Nordic doctor with an Ellen DeGeneres haircut and Banana Republic "man slacks" was threatening to pump my stomach. The interaction went something like this:

"Ve haf to pump your stomach."

"No fucking way." I was adamant and out of my head.

"You took a lot of medication and alcohol."

"I'm not even unconscious and it's been over an hour. I'm not going to die. I'm just really fucked up. You know I'm not going to die."

She looked me dead in the eye. "Ver you trying to kavill yourself?"

"Until my wife interrupted me! Hell yeah! But she fucked it all up!" I was so furious at Debra. I was planning on screaming at her for calling 911 as soon as I saw her. I hated her for this. "Where the fuck is she?"

"She's not allowed in here right now. And that's enov to put you on a 72-hour hold." She seemed glib.

"What is a 72-hour hold?" I sat up straight on the bed. The intravenous tubes connected to my arms pulled me back down.

"You'll be in da psych vard for 72 hours for valuation. Noting you can do about it. It's fer your vown savety. You'll be valuated by doctor."

All I could do was shout, "fuck!" Never say you are trying to kill yourself. Automatic 72-hour hold. I never made that mistake again. No matter how hard they try and get you to say it, keep your fucking mouth shut. Otherwise they've got you.

So I tried to disconnect myself from the IVs and started spurting blood like a fire hydrant out of my arm. Two doctors came in and patched me up. They were actually very nice and non-antagonistic. It made me feel a little less aggressive. I hated that Nordic doctor. She had no compassion. I could tell she thought that since I "did this to myself," I was dirt.

But then they brought in two flunky guards to make sure I stayed connected and in place. They were wearing polyester floods and the elastic in their socks was shot so they were rolling down, exposing ankle. What a sorry bunch they were. Is this the kind of job you get when you go to vocational school to be in law enforcement I wondered? Did they think they were going to be FBI agents based on a commercial they saw on daytime TV?

Next a male nurse brought in the charcoal that was supposed to neutralize what was in my stomach and I refused to drink it. I drank it in Philadelphia once and I shit grey liquid in my hospital gown uncontrollably.

I screamed "Never again!" like the Jews said about the Nazi genocide in World War II. I got the joke. Nobody else did. I thought it was funny.

I was in that room behind a curtain for what seemed an eternity. Finally when they were sure I wasn't going to die, the armed guards with the high water slacks escorted me upstairs to the locked psych ward, one holding each arm. As they escorted me up I saw my wife Debra and told her to go fuck herself for doing this to me as the elevator doors slammed shut. She was crying.

Debra was only doing what she thought best, never in her life having dealt with something like this. She thought she was saving my life. She loved me. She couldn't just let me die, even if I ended up hating her. This whole thing was out of her realm. But at the time all I could think about was that I couldn't go home for three days.

Until that moment, my wife had not really known me. She knew I suffered from depression, but she never saw what it did to me. I never had an incident while I was with her up to that point. And I'd never really told her everything about how I grew up. Yes, bits and pieces. But I had never put it all together into something that made sense, so how was I going to explain it to her?

According to protocol, they put you in the severe side of the ward until they can evaluate you. It was late at night so I ended up in one of those locked rooms with the observation window, but they didn't lock the door. The roommate I was paired with was snoring so loud I couldn't take it and this was the only other option. But being in this room stressed me out so much I was up all night anyway. My mind was racing a mile a minute. I kept wondering what kind of psychos had been strapped down to this very bed and locked in this room before me. I wondered if they pissed the bed and I was lying in a big stain.

The next morning I emerged into the hallway in my hospital gown. I had no direction whatsoever where to go or what to do. I found my way into a day room where about seven people in various states of delusion were watching static on a television set. I didn't know if they were talking to me, themselves, each other or what. They were all just talking and none of it made sense. All I wanted to do was scream at my wife.

I tried to talk to them but nothing they said made sense. This seemed too severe a place for me. Was I this bad off that I needed to be in this environment? Was I this crazy that I belonged with them? When I spoke did I make no sense? Was there actually something on TV and I just saw static? I was really getting worried. Plus I hadn't had my Elavil and I was starting to get the shakes.

I walked out to the nurse's station. A nurse seemed to know me. One of those middle aged, motherly "I've got it all under control" types with the big breasts.

"Mr. Goodman, your wife brought some clothes by for you. You can change out of the gown if you like. And we are going to transfer you to the other side where there are less restrictions and it's a little less scary." She handed me my gym bag from home. I couldn't believe even the nurse was telling me this place was scary. I felt vindicated. But I still wanted out of there ASAP.

"Thank god." I mumbled. "I thought I was this crazy."

She laughed. "I know it's a little intense over here. The other side is much better, but they have to start you out over here to make sure you're okay for the other side."

So I went into someone's room and changed into the street clothes Debra had dropped off and I felt a little better. Two guys in the room liked my shirt and actually asked me if they could have it. It was obvious from their looks and smell they were homeless. I told them I needed it.

Getting my own clothes also made me a little less angry with Debra for some reason. Like she did care and wasn't just having me locked up because she couldn't deal with me.

Finally someone came and got me and took me to the "other side." It was still a locked ward, but the patients were a little more coherent. And I was lucky enough to get a room without a roommate. I called Debra on the pay phone to scream at her but I couldn't. She did what she thought was best. She thought I was going to kill myself and she loved me. So I acknowledged her feelings and decided I had no right to be angry. She cried and said she was so glad I understood. Then I bitched that it was mid-afternoon and I had not seen a doctor or had any medication and was feeling pretty bad.

So I sat in the day room waiting for a doctor, becoming more and more uncomfortable. Finally someone came and took me to see my new doctor. This doctor was really young and beautiful, as was her assistant. Both were younger than I, which was a little embarrassing at first. But they were very sweet to me and apologized for the long wait. The doctor's name was Tammy. How hot was that? Even at my worst my penis was becoming partially alive.

We talked a lot about my history and Tammy noted that I not only suffered from depression, but that I had hypomanic episodes, which meant I actually went up and down. And in my case, it was very rapid cycling. I could complete a cycle in several minutes. But, the main thing I struggled with was depression. She felt I was bipolar II.

I couldn't believe it. She hit me dead on. Sometimes I could be completely depressed and hopeless, and then I'd make a sale at work and be giddy with delight and sky high. Eventually I got so exhausted from being up I crashed. But this could happen suddenly several times a day. Or, the cycles could last a week.

I was utterly relieved. After thirteen years of being diagnosed as severely depressed a doctor finally addressed all my symptoms and nailed it spot on. Doctor Tammy felt I was misdiagnosed as depressed and needed a specific bipolar drug like Lithium or Depakote. Lithium is actually a kind of salt found naturally in the body.

However, Doctor Tammy was going by what the book said with very little practical experience of her own. I had tried Lithium before and it made me more depressed and bloated so she decided to put me on Depakote. And because I was in the hospital they could give me huge doses very quickly and monitor my blood daily to speed things along. She said she couldn't tell me how long I'd be here but it definitely would be more than seventy-two hours. I agreed to hang in there as long as it took.

I thanked her and was ready to get started. I wanted to get well. It seemed Dr. Munster didn't know any of this protocol. Maybe if he had, all this could have been avoided. And Doctor Tammy was so attractive *and* seemed to know everything about the latest treatments. I kept hoping she'd need to grab my testicles and ask me to cough or something.

So I started on Depakote and killed time waiting for it to work. But this side of the psych ward was not all it was cracked up to be, to risk sounding cliché.

First there was a guy who was trying to grow breasts and who always used the women's bathroom. He only gave me dirty looks. For some reason he did not like me. He'd never return my "hello" or thanked me if I took a message for him from the pay phone. I kept thinking, "Buddy, take a look at yourself, you're lucky I'm not laughing."

Then there was a gay middle-aged man with anger issues who decided we were going to be best friends. All he wanted to do was sit in my room and talk about his gayness and his lover who had spurned him from his life for no reason that he could possibly fathom. Down in L.A. he had a fabulous home with his lover and all kinds of cars. He just had this anger problem. But I liked hanging around with him, he was coherent and you could have an intelligent conversation with him. And when he'd lose his temper with the staff sometimes they'd call security, which kept life interesting.

Then there was the Vietnam vet who lived in the Tenderloin of San Francisco with his toothless girlfriend. For some reason I never learned why he ended up in the psych ward. I'm not sure what his issue was but his body seemed to be failing. Every time he went into the men's room to take a dump he would let out this sorrowful moan and it sounded as if his innards were chunkily dropping out of his body into the toilet, making huge splashdowns. Kidneys and everything. I doubt he lived through the year.

The person who interested me most was a shorthaired blond schizophrenic girl about my age. Her face seemed to be so hardened she almost had a harsh five o'clock shadow, but yet there was something attractive about her. We talked a lot but I could tell she was fighting something. One night she sat outside the nurse's station crying hysterically. The nurses seemed to be paying her no mind. They were immune to patients in crisis; they didn't call the doctor for every "little thing," so I got down on my knees next to her and asked if she wanted me to sit with her. I wanted to know if talking with her was making it worse or better in her head. I knew she was hearing voices. She said me talking with her was making it worse so I left her alone, but it tore me apart inside. I went into my room and cried for her. She didn't deserve that. And nobody seemed to be helping her. To the best of my knowledge nobody was even calling her doctor. Everyone had the attitude that she does this all the time. It was no big deal. Well, I'm sure to her it was. I guess it was just another day at the office.

The entire hospital experience was discouraging. Unless you were meeting with your doctor, you were subject to the most ridiculous activities and rules. It was like you were being punished for being mentally ill. No TV after 10:00 P.M., you could only watch certain shows and you had to go to these demoralizing activities or else stay in your room. You really were in prison, locked doors and all. And I was not sleeping. I lay in my bed every night trying so hard but I could not drift off. And finally when they gave me something to help me sleep I'd have tiny little periods of slumber with horrific nightmares, and then I'd be up for hours trying to calm myself down. And you couldn't go into the other room and turn on the TV. I was too tired to read. Listening to music gave me a headache. So you just remained miserable in this stark room.

My favorite demoralization was practically being forced to go to music therapy. I was sitting in a room with two very delusional men and a perfectly sane Vietnam vet. This one looked like Willem Dafoe from *Platoon* and we had talked a little bit about his experiences in the rec area. He was very sane, just an addict.

A small-framed, towheaded volunteer from San Francisco State and his candy-ass sidekick came in with an acoustic guitar and wanted us to have a sing along. They thought it would be therapeutic and were obviously getting some kind of academic credit for it. So they start playing Cat Stevens's "Father and Son" as if we'd never heard it before and tried to teach us the significance of the words.

I'd known that song my entire life and they were probably three when it came out. The vet probably hummed the tune in Saigon as he shooting a machine gun from his chopper in 1970. Yet this little nineteen-year-old college student was trying to turn us on to it as if it's new music. His music. The vet and I locked eyes and I could see the laughter in them. He loved the irony. But I didn't think it was very funny. I thought it was disrespectful. I told the little guitar playing asshole to go fuck himself and walked out. I hated people like him. And being locked in a psych ward wasn't going to make me change.

The vet stayed and kept singing. Maybe he was tired of fighting. Maybe my illness was magnifying the situation in my head. But it's what I felt at the time so I couldn't just sit there and take it. It became a cause, a matter of principle. I was nobody's fool.

Then there was an arts and crafts class. I forget what we were making, but some severely mentally ill people from the other side were there and were misappropriating glue. They just couldn't focus and do the project properly. And believe it or not the art therapist yelled at them. I couldn't believe it! I mean what did they expect? These people were not well. I felt compelled to say something to the matron teaching the class.

"Look, give them a break. They are doing the best they can. They can't help themselves. You don't have to yell at them."

And the matron who had obviously been in the system way too long said, "Mr. Goodman, am I going to have a problem with you too? You need to behave yourself and work on your project. Sundays are very lonely to spend in your room."

And I replied, "It's easy to be nasty to people who can't fight back. Spending the afternoon in my room sounds pretty good right now to me and a lot better than doing your fucking little art project." And off I went to my room. I never heard her reply. I just wanted out of this prison. My seventy-two hours were long up, even though Dr. Tammy said it would take longer than that to help me feel better. *Legally* I was allowed out if I was not deemed a threat to myself.

The problem was I still felt like shit. The medication was not working. It didn't feel right in my body. I had the shakes and I was depressed. And every time I told my doctor she said it was because the Depakote was not up to a therapeutic level in my bloodstream. But I am one of those people who know if something is going to work right away. And this felt wrong.

I had been there for a week and I couldn't take it anymore. My wife visited every day. I told her the Depakote wasn't right, that I was still depressed and had horrible anxiety. I needed to get out and meet with Dr. Munster and balance things out with an antidepressant or something. Dr. Tammy wanted me to stay until I achieved the right levels in my bloodstream, but she refused to concede that this was the wrong medication. I was beginning to feel she had her head stuck in a textbook.

Debra came on a Saturday and I told her I was going to say I felt better and push for a Monday release. I knew they couldn't hold me any longer. And I wanted out before the doctor could get involved. Debra was against it at first, thinking I would go back to being suicidal. I assured I wouldn't. That I would go right to Dr. Munster and get straightened out. She agreed to trust me and went along with my wishes.

I was going to bust out of there even if she didn't agree. I had it all figured out. Someone would open the ward door; I'd be dressed, grab my backpack and take the stairs to the next floor down and then run along the corridor to the far end of the building and catch the elevator. Everyone would be chasing me down the stairwell and I'd be on the elevator. I'd walk right out the far side lobby instead of the main one. When I hit the street I'd head for home via cab, get my car and then take off to a hotel where I could sort things out and take a long hot shower to wash the institution off of me.

On a Saturday I started telling the nurses how great I felt and to start the paperwork because I was leaving on Monday morning. The truth was I felt like I was jumping out of my skin and was depressed out of my mind all at the same time. Another mixed-state. It's a hallmark for individuals with bipolar II. Someone was playing tug-of-war with my brain and every nerve in my body was in knots. But I wasn't getting any better in the hospital and first thing Monday morning the attending physician had to sign off on the paperwork. I wasn't suicidal and I passed the 72-hour hold days ago. I was out on the street before Dr. Tammy even knew I was planning on leaving. I was glad I didn't have to go fugie.

Weeks later when I was out of the hospital and back at work, I went into a record store in downtown San Francisco during lunch to buy a CD. This schizophrenic girl from the hospital was now the checkout girl. We recognized each other and laughed. I had so much respect for her that I wanted to hug her and burst into tears. I knew how hard it was for her just to get up in the morning and fight past the voices telling her terrible things about herself. I told her she looked wonderful, I hoped she was doing well and that it made my day to see her. I think it made her happy to know somebody understood and appreciated what she went through. Obviously it was a secret. I thought to myself, "Man, whenever you think you have it bad, somebody has it worse." I wondered how "budding breast boy" was doing.

So when I got out of the hospital I went back to Dr. Munster. He wasn't the most sophisticated on medications. Also like Herman Munster, he never wanted to upset his wife Lily, which in this case was the Medical Board, by doling out too much of anything at one time. He needed a Grandpa who would go down into his dungeon laboratory and mix up the good stuff, turning me into Jackie Gleason.

Then I could always be the life of the party and have plenty of money to throw around. And if I got depressed I'd have a doctor on a payroll fix me up with a shot of something or other and I'd be fine in no time. I loved Jackie Gleason. He was a pool shark, comedian, gambler, entertainer and everyone loved to be around him. And when he wasn't being Ralph Kramden, the man knew how to dress with a pencil thin moustache and a silk handkerchief in his coat pocket. This is how I am. In the middle of a crisis thinking about fat Jackie Gleason.

However, Munster did get me on a mood stabilizer that agreed with me and on an antidepressant. I was finally being treated for both my mania and depression. The downer was I never again felt as good as I did on Elavil. Elavil, when it worked, kept me in a constant state of excitement, thrills and chills. I could break into laughter just out of a feeling of contentment. Now I was mourning its loss. Not even steadily increasing the dosage could revive my old friend Ellie. I needed a new antidepressant *and* a mood stabilizer to keep me even. I was definitely bipolar. An antidepressant alone was not going to cut it.

The problem was, life started to suck now that I was being treated for the right illness with mood stabilizers. Everything was just blah for me after that. I couldn't get really excited about anything, nor could I get really sad about anything. I just existed. It's then when I learned the joys of drinking with my medication. Anything to give me a little lift. Otherwise, life was completely flat for me. Sex was flat. Music was flat. Movies were flat. Work was flat. Life was just going through the motions.

I knew I was going to have other episodes in my life because I couldn't live like this. No pill could keep me down. But I did learn my lesson about the 72-hour hold. No matter what you do to yourself, never say you are trying to commit suicide to the police, EMTs or attending physicians in the emergency room. If you don't say it, the worst they can do is make you sleep it off overnight with the drunks and addicts and give you cab fare home in the morning. Since then I've been complimented numerous times on how well I chose my words whenever I found myself in a hospital emergency room.

And all I can say is that nobody ever got well locked in a psych ward being treated like an idiot while being experimented on by medical students. Our mentally ill are not criminals. They are to be respected. Their wounds are so painful they can't be bandaged or eased with pain-killers. Nobody can promise them recovery or assuage their fears. The mentally ill can be in the most technologically advanced hospital and they might as well be in a medieval torture chamber. They feel fear and despair and long for relief that may never come. Yet our mental wards and institutions treat them like nuisances and give them sarcastic, unsympathetic and lazy caregivers instead of compassionate and caring professionals. I can't find words powerful enough to explain how this egregious neglect and indifference affects me on an emotional level, in or outside of a mental ward. It never leaves me.

I hope Dr. Tammy gained some real world experience and learned to get her head out of the book and into her patients' heads. Or at least into her patients' laps. Something good has to come out of being one of her patients.

Sales Jobs, Con Jobs and Blowjobs

I remember sitting in a sales meeting at a classical music radio station in my early twenties in Philadelphia with my sales manager, introducing a new radio commercial package I was expected to sell at least one of in the next four weeks. I already felt like I wanted to run away and hide where nobody could see me. I looked around the room at the other sales people and they all looked so professional and put together. I knew they would have no trouble pulling this off. Some would probably sell two. I fought back the urge to cry as the tears welled up in my eye sockets. This is the sales job.

The women were all wearing bright colored suits, short skirts, bright colored silk scarves wrapped around their necks and loads of perfume that made my eyes burn. But the burning felt good in a weird kind of way. And I knew they were going to have no trouble selling these packages. I wanted to buy one from them on the secret hope that they'd have sex with me. I knew that's why their customers did, even if it was subconsciously.

All the men had on double-breasted suits, ties with colorful floral patterns painted on them, matching handkerchiefs and those tiny leather toe loafers with the tassels. They looked slick. I knew they'd each be able to easily finesse their sales quotas from fresh, young post-college coeds on their first media buying assignment and cougar media queens who loved the attention from anything with a penis and an expense account.

And there I was, in one of my three suits. This was a dark brown single-breaster with a green shirt and green patterned tie with brown penny loafers. I mean it all matched and looked modern, but I was not sharp or refined. And all I could think was why did I pick a dark brown suit and green shirt and tie? Moreover, my medication made my mouth bone dry, my hands shake. I was sweating and I thought everyone could see I was close to falling apart. I found it hard enough to keep myself together, let alone pay attention to my sales manager's rhetoric.

The rest of the day I was cold-calling businesses I found in the phonebook or newspaper and magazine ads trying to get appointments to sell them this "amazing radio advertising package" I had to move at least one of. Only I didn't know how to qualify a prospect, what to say to get an appointment, how to answer objections, how to get through to a decision maker or even gauge whether it was a good call or not. And when I was given the opportunity to make my pitch I was so nervous I sounded like a boy scout trying to sell raffle tickets to win a lawn mower.

I literally started calling local Burger Kings, asking fifteen-year-old inner city counter girls who made their advertising decisions and whether they would like to advertise on my classical music radio station? All they heard was the word radio and thought I was a DJ calling to put them on the local rap radio station and started screaming "hey" to their mommas and dedicating Run DMC songs to their delinquent boyfriends.

I had no clue about demographics and ad agencies that handled major accounts like Burger King. I just heard Burger King on another radio station so I thought I'd call a local franchise and see about getting them on the air. I figured people who liked Bach still ate burgers, so why not? I was going to be a renegade. I could only imagine the laughter the other sales people in my office were trying to repress when they heard me stumbling and fumbling on the phone with national accounts with which I didn't stand a chance.

After a couple of weeks of no appointments and pressure from management to get on the street, I started making a list of businesses to just walk in on and ask to see the owner. So there I went in my turd-brown suit and 1989 Plymouth Sundance, driving all over the Philadelphia Metropolitan area calling on chain stores who obviously made their advertising decisions in Minnesota, or small merchants who couldn't even afford to print a flyer and stick it on a windshield. And I'd walk in asking them to spend five grand on a classical music radio station.

Sometimes people would tell me maybe in a month to give them a call just to get me out of their store. So, I'd drive ninety miles per hour back to the station to tell my sales manager I practically had an order. And at the end of the month when I stopped by to "close the deal" the merchant didn't even remember me. It was like a dagger in my heart. "Oh Spartacus, I have been dealt a mighty death blow. Finish me off, I beg of ye!"

I constantly thought to myself, "Why did I think I could do this job? I am not like other people. I can't handle something like sales. I'm a pole. Maybe I should set my sights lower. Maybe I can't work at all. Should I be on disability? Instead of calling on Burger Kings, should I be flipping burgers at one? No goals. No quotas. No competition. No wardrobe. Just a polyester uniform like everyone else and a zit-faced thirty-five year old manager trying to work his way up the corporate ladder explaining to me how to use the fry machine. And I'm sure I could figure that out. As a matter of fact, if I showed up for work on time and did my job without complaining I'd probably make it to the register and actually get to deal with customers. Wasn't that kind of like sales? 'Sir, how about fries with that Whopper?' "

And how could I fuck up taking an order for a Whopper and fries? Scratch that, I'd probably make the wrong change and get busted back down to the fryer. Then I'd have to put this on my resume and never get on the counter again in the fast food game. And let me tell you, there is no glory on the fry machine. Don't let anyone ever tell you differently.

Then one day I'd have breathed so much grease that I'd get too sick to work, the company would turn me out and I would die an early death. My family would get nothing from the company. And my kids were probably working on a fryer at another Burger King because that was all they knew and were going to die the same horrible, crispy death. Or, maybe I'd grow some balls and become the Norma Rae of fast food French fry makers and stand up on the counter of a Burger King with a cardboard sign demanding better working conditions for this group of downtrodden greasers.

A circus of thoughts like this went through my mind every day when the alarm went off and it was time to go to work. And it went on this way for years. Even as I got better at my job, stopped buying brown suits and learned not to call on franchise stores, I was having trouble with my medication. Side effects, losing a sale, never making enough money, not measuring up to my peers or a plethora of others things would unexpectedly throw me into a psychological tailspin which I found very hard to control. And all the while I had to fake normalcy at work in front of my coworkers, management, prospects and clients. I would lie in bed almost every night and wonder why it had to be so hard for me and not for anybody else.

Then I would remember this girl in college. It was pouring rain one morning and I was sitting in an 8:30 A.M. class pissed that my leather jacket was soaked and my hair looked like shit. I think it had curled up from the humidity, making me look like I had horns. Plus my feet were wet, I was tired, hung-over and just in a general bad mood from my predicament.

Suddenly a girl in my class came in operating her wheel chair with this device in her mouth because she could not use her arms. She had a big tarp over her to keep the rain off and it was drenched. She rolled into an empty space next to a friend who helped her get set up for class and pulled off the tarp. She was smiling and I heard her say she took the bus in from wherever she lived in the city. Based on her quadriplegic condition, I was sure she also had to undergo the humiliation of wearing a diaper. Yet she had a smile on her face, books in front of her and was just making normal conversation with her neighbors. She was going about life the best she could and wasn't even feeling sorry for herself. In fact, she seemed happy to be there.

I wanted to sucker-punch myself, but I couldn't catch myself off guard. I thought, "What is my problem? Why do I feel sorry for myself because my hair has horns and my feet are wet? Shame on me: this girl probably had to get up at four o'clock this morning to make it to class on time because it takes her forever to do the simplest tasks. She's drenched, can't do a damn thing about the way she looks, rode a hot, sweaty city bus yet she's smiling and ready for class. I have no right to complain. I walked to class on my own two feet and didn't even appreciate it. She just appreciates being able to make it to class."

And from that day on, whenever I'm feeling really sorry for myself due to inconveniences of nature or just bad luck, I try to remind myself of this girl from college and how she had it worse but took it with grace. It doesn't always work, like when my car was stolen and the Philadelphia police gave me a ticket for parking it in an empty lot in North Philadelphia where it had been dumped and stripped. As if I intentionally drove it there, dismantled it and left its pathetic skeleton for the neighborhood kids to climb on like a jungle gym. But it does make me think twice and adjust my attitude a little.

Back to the sales job. A lot of people who are not bipolar can't or won't do sales. They don't like cold-calling, making presentations, the rejection, the repetitive nature and other things required to master the occupation. And there is absolutely nothing wrong with that. There are some days I ask why I subjected myself to such a horrid profession. It's the only one I know of that makes you question your sense of worth on a daily, sometimes hourly basis. But over the years I have become accustomed to it.

However, there a lot of jobs out there that I don't think I could handle and find sales much more preferable to. For instance, I'd cut my throat if I had to work in an office all day and never get out. Or sit in front of a computer doing programming. I'd hate Human Resources where I'd have to deal with employee issues, like who pulled whose hair. And I could never take having to be an attorney and knowing all those rules of law. But there are a hell of a lot of people who would rather do these things than be out on the street getting rejected all day and having their income depend on whether people liked you or not.

But what I can't take is people who use their bipolar illness as an excuse not to do *anything*. Of course there are many cases where people can't regulate their moods and it's blatantly obvious they can't survive in a workplace environment, but a lot of people who are on permanent disability are in fact actually working; they're on the con.

Notice I say "permanent disability." There are times with bipolar illness when medications are being changed or you have some kind of crisis and time off is needed. I've been there. Thank god for the federal Family and Medical Leave Act. Luckily for me I've only needed financial support for a couple of weeks at a time. But for some people it might be a year or two. Everyone recovers at his or her own rate. Some don't. You can't put a timetable on it.

But there are a lot of bipolars I have come in contact with who are milking the system so hard they're making cream. This is the con job. They can work but have either convinced themselves they can't or are too lazy to try. And when I heard someone on permanent disability tell someone aspiring to such a status in a support group I attended, "You are almost always turned down the first time you apply. But don't worry, almost everyone eventually gets it," I spewed venom because I chose not to be on the con and force myself to work. And I don't think that was the kind of support the group was intended to supply.

The woman in my support group who doled out this sagely advice was in her fifties and on permanent disability, called SSDI in California, because she was angry at her ex-husband who was a pot head. Apparently he wouldn't admit it and everyone still loved him and thought she was a crab. The fact that he was a phony made her infuriated for so many years that she found a doctor to convince Social Security to pay her monthly disability for the rest of her life. Her doctor should be a lawyer if he can convince anyone of that.

Another woman in the group was there for every meeting. She wasn't bipolar, or at least never complained or spoke of any symptoms. I also knew she did not take any medication. And she never shared anything about herself. But I did know she hadn't worked for years and had run out of government assistance. She was very sympathetic to others in the group and a strong advocate for lying around on your ass if you could possibly get away with it.

Her specialty was befriending others in the group with very serious issues. She'd become part of their lives for a few months, even inviting them into her home and then they'd suddenly disappear. In my tenure at the group I counted three very ill members suddenly vanish. I was afraid to even sit next to her in the big circle.

The other thing she was good at was organizing groups to go out to eat after each meeting. Eventually she started bringing people home to her lair for cooking parties after meetings. Only certain people were invited, though. I think it was based on level of sickness. "The sicker, the tastier," I thought whenever my mind drifted to the group members no longer with us.

It's not that she wasn't a kind person, she just reminded me of a frog. She'd sit in the meetings and let her neck fill up with air and then croak out some words of encouragement for people now and then. She seemed to be feeding off everyone's misery. And although she was compassionate, I couldn't figure out why she was in the group, unless she was aspiring to be mentally ill. And when it came to free government services, this woman was *Britannica Junior.*

The final example of abusing the system was the group facilitator. A very nice man in his thirties who suffered from debilitating depression. He was on complete disability. He also had a problem with making mean comments to people he didn't like. The problem was, they were often complete strangers.

But for someone on complete disability, he did more volunteer work and things of personal interest requiring greater concentration and effort than a regular fulltime job. He was constantly on the move with one commitment or the other. If the government was looking for cutbacks, he could be of service to his country and just *try* working. Or at least stop verbally accosting strangers for no reason at all. I know. It's hard for me, too. But that's what the internet is for.

Here's what I have to say to all the capable bipolars I have met in person and online who tell me they can't work with creative excuses, like, "I can't help taking over and telling the boss how to run the business," "I get in a fight with all the customers," and "none of the other workers like me because I don't want to talk to anyone." And my favorite: "I need too many special accommodations, such as I can't work regular hours, I need frequent breaks, sometimes I just have to stop what I'm doing and lie down and I can't handle any type of pressure." I shit you not, real people have said these things to me in group.

I'm sure the people who have these criteria believe it, but it's nonsense. The truth is that everyone wants to tell their boss how not to fuck up their business, but he/she is the boss and entitled to drive their business into the ground any way they see fit. So unless they have a suggestion box or are asking for your advice, keep it to yourself. They aren't interested in hearing it. And since they own the business and you are probably just an admin, they know more than you do, anyway. So keep it to yourself as long as you are getting paid.

And arguing with customers is completely under your own control. Some customers can be obnoxious. But be an adult, let the customer always be right and let it go. Then, when you go home that night, send a transvestite hooker to their house. Believe me, they'll treat everyone a little nicer after that. Screaming at them in the workplace will do nothing but get you fired.

Moreover, if you think everyone always hates you in the workplace, it's probably because they do. Try showing an interest in others and talk to them, even if you couldn't care less. Maybe compliment someone once in a while? This has nothing to do with your mental illness. It's just your sorry-ass attitude. Fix it. It's so simple.

Finally, for those of you who think you can't work because you need all these special accommodations: it's all in your head and not the part that needs to be medicated. You're probably going to be working at the Gap, so it's not a pressure-packed job like being an air traffic controller. There is plenty of downtime, you never have to work in the middle of the night and you can always lie down in the stockroom on a pile of last year's flat-front chinos and nobody will even know you're missing. Everyone looks the same there. You can handle a four- or eight-hour shift with lunch, dinner and other half-hour breaks just like everyone else. Remember, you're folding sweaters all day, not working on a chain gang in Kentucky.

But the ridiculous excuses for getting lifetime disability for mental illness isn't the end of the government con job. If you're on permanent SSDI in California the most you're probably getting is $3,000 a month. Of course you get food stamps, MediCal, etc., but the fact of the matter is you are not getting rich – unless you're working on the side. I have met several individuals on disability who admitted they were earning income on the side. Once you're approved, the system is fairly lax and if you're careful it's not hard to do. Especially with things like eBay and Craigslist beckoning you.

Those on SSDI who really score are people whose spouses have good jobs or live with financially secure partners or parents. Then all the money they get from the government for permanent disability is just gravy on them biscuits. It's an extra $2,000-3,000 a month and free medical for someone who is already being taken care of.

I met a guy in his thirties on the internet in a bipolar chat room living in rural Pennsylvania with his parents. No question about it, he had severe mental issues. But a lot of them were because he was hooked on painkillers, speed and weed. He was on permanent disability so his parents set him up in a room at home with the best computer and audio-video equipment money could buy. When he got bored with his movies, internet friends and music he'd take his government check and use it to buy drugs from his neighbor and then go on a binge. The money was pure surplus. I think if his parents kicked him out of the playpen he might be doing a lot better with less disposable income.

This brings us to the blowjob. It's basically what happens to all bipolars, whether we decide to forge ahead into the working world or sit it out on the sidelines on disability. Either way you suffer. If you work you have to try and meld into society while dealing with mood swings, medications, side effects and feelings of despair. And if you take the government option, you wonder what you could have been and have done for the rest your life. With the second option I have to believe you wake up every day wondering if you made the right decision by opting not to work. No matter what you do if you suffer from bipolar illness, you're screwed. It's the big blowjob.

You're not like anyone else and are relegated to a life of constantly being conscious of your mental status and what you need to do to regulate it to function in society. Eventually for most of us it becomes second nature, but I think the non-bipolar community would definitely be overwhelmed if they knew the mental stopgaps we must engage in just to get through the day.

I know I seem judgmental of those of us who have *decided* not to work and take advantage of lifelong disability. And although I do think there are a lot of bipolar as well as other mentally ill people out there shaking down the system for a free ride, I believe everyone who ends up on the government payroll has a come-to-Jesus moment sooner or later about what their life has become that isn't all that pleasant. And if they're capable of working but play the system, they will live in their own special hell with their $2,000-3,000 a month for the rest of their lives. If they legitimately can't work, I hope they feel safely wrapped in the American flag, which protects those of us who truly can't work with the contributions of those who can.

I'll bet there were a couple of Republicans out there getting erections when they thought I was bashing the mentally ill for being on government disability. I'm just criticizing those who can work and take the easy way out. Because, I walked around in a brown suit cold-calling fast food chains for advertising dollars looking like a complete dope.

Pass It On

Debra and I tried to have sex and get her pregnant like a normal couple. But after a year that wasn't happening. And as with any loving couple she blamed me and forced me to have my sperm tested. So I went to the clinic and was asked to masturbate into a cup. As my luck would have it no jerk off rooms were available and the attractive receptionist-coordinator asked me if I wouldn't mind doing it in the bathroom. So I took the specimen cup in front of the entire waiting room, went into the men's room and locked the door. I lay down on the dirty tile floor and thought about how everyone knew what I was doing. I think the humiliation of it actually turned me on a little.

Then I meekly brought out my manhood in a jar concealed in a paper bag so the whole world didn't have to see, and handed it to the receptionist. But the entire waiting room knew what I had just done and what was in the bag. As I stood there she peeked inside as if I might have gotten confused in the men's room and shit in the cup instead. I was so glad when she took it off my hands, labeled it and told me I could go. I got out of there as fast as possible. "On a bathroom floor!" I thought. They made it seem so foul. "Why didn't they just ask me to go in the janitor's closet and masturbate into an empty bottle of Mr. Clean?"

Anyway, much to my surprise it turned out I had an awesome sperm count. I was actually blown away because, after all the medication I'd pumped into my body over the years, I expected my sperm was being pushed around on hospital stretchers in a psychiatric dayroom in my balls and just languishing there moaning for their meds all day. But apparently I was shooting some healthy rounds. Frankly, I was astonished because I still only had limited sensation from the drug side effects. I figured something had to be wrong with my sperm count.

So now it was on my wife, which turned out not to be worthy of the victory dance. According to the doctor, we had to start having sex when her body temperature was at a specific level right before her period. This meant she'd call me at the office, I'd have to rush home, have sex whether I felt like it or not, and then she'd stand on her head for an hour to make sure my men made their way into her ovaries. It got to the point I'd cringe when the phone rang at work and I saw her number come up. I was beginning to hate sex. It was completely mechanical and unromantic.

This went on for a year. And, each time we did it I became more disenchanted with wanting to have a biological child. I had always been a proponent of adoption. I was feeling terribly guilty that I would pass on my bipolar illness, which is something I wasn't sure I could live with. Moreover, I didn't want to pass along my vision impairment and shifty eyes, either. This, too, is hereditary. I kept thinking to myself, "What the fuck am I doing? I'll never forgive myself if my child gets either one of these afflictions. Then my opinion on right and wrong will mean nothing. I have to take a stand for what I believe in."

Debra and I had discussed adoption before. I finally brought it up again. I told her two years of trying was enough. Maybe there was a message here that this was not the right thing to do. Why take a chance on having a mentally ill and/or visually impaired child when there are so many kids in the world about to be born and who need parents? And Debra, being the intelligent woman that she was, gave up her innate hopes of having her own biological child and decided to get fully behind adoption. I think giving up on pregnancy was one of the hardest things she ever had to do. I'll never stop respecting her for doing what she thought was right, and not for what she yearned for as a woman. And many men want the "full fatherhood experience" as well, even though they aren't the ones throwing up for nine months until they are stretched and cut open to give birth to a cannon ball.

So, in 1998 we started the adoption process. And the entire time, through all the FBI background checks and home visits to qualify us as acceptable adoptive parents, I thought my bipolar history was going to blow the whole thing out of the water. During each interview I just waited for the other shoe to drop when the interviewer would turn to me and say, "Mr. Goodman, you've been in a locked mental ward several times for bipolar illness. You take a bevy of psychotropic medications. You've attempted suicide on numerous occasions. Not only can't you adopt a child, but we are taking away your cats."

But it didn't work that way. We were counseled to be straight up with any potential birthmother about my illness if asked, and not to say anything at all if it didn't come up. Apparently the agency we chose felt it was not a deal killer or something that we had to disclose up front. After about a thousand interviews they had really gotten to know us as a couple and felt we were more than fit prospective parents. I couldn't help but think I must have really fooled them. I could not picture myself as a parent. I kept envisioning myself fighting with my five-year-old over who got to watch what on TV.

In my mind I never stopped worrying about it. And what if we were meeting with a birthmother and it came up that I was mentally ill? Who in their right mind would want me as a father for their child? The irrational fear that Debra could be bringing me home from the psych ward the same day as our new baby from the maternity ward haunted me. This made the entire process especially nerve-racking.

Amazingly, it was over in six months from the time we actually put ourselves on the market as approved adoptive parents. It all started with a brochure I put together about Debra and me for prospective birthmothers.

I am in advertising, so I do know how to promote. I didn't just write a description of us as prospective parents, I went all out and wrote full blown advertising copy with pictures in a tri-folding four color brochure. This is my profession and I marketed Debra and myself unabashedly.

I just didn't know how well. We had a birthmother contact us within a month of our brochure being available. An adoption counselor showed it to a prospective birthmother in Nevada and she chose us practically before we even met. Debra and I were not prepared for this to happen so quickly. She was on a temporary work assignment on the east coast and had to fly back to California on a day's notice so we could go to Nevada and meet the birthmother.

The meeting was surreal. We met the twenty-one-year-old at a diner in a small town in Nevada. She barely looked pregnant. She told us her Marlboro-man father was in the diner, too, at the counter so to just pretend we were giving her a job interview to work at our ranch in San Francisco. Obviously she had never been to San Francisco or she'd realize it's not a big ranching city. The whole thing was bizarre.

Naturally Debra had about 450 questions to ask and plenty of nervous premature laughter that sounded like a machine gun. But it was obvious to us the girl's mind was made up and half an hour later we were giving her directions to our apartment in the city. She said she'd be there the following Saturday and was due in about five weeks.

A week later we had a pick-up-driving, pregnant twenty-one-year-old country girl and her mangy herding dog living in our San Francisco apartment's spare bedroom. I tried to find her an apartment nearby but there was nothing nice where I felt she'd be comfortable.

So for five weeks I had to be on my best behavior twenty-four hours a day so she wouldn't pull out on us. We had to be the perfect family. No farting, arguing or drinking too much and I was hiding my pills everywhere. Every night after dinner I tried to pretend I was reading a book but all I wanted to do was watch *Big Brother* on TV. Plus, Debra was pissing me off by overdoing it with the mothering of the birthmother. She was the undisputed queen of taking everything to the max. It was like we had a twenty-one-year-old daughter.

Debra took the birthmother on a hospital tour so she could see where she was going to give birth. Then they looked at all the birthing rooms and Debra went about the process of trying to secure the one she liked best, as if it were a hotel. She inspected every instrument, tube and bedpan that was going to be part of the procedure.

Then came the visiting nurse Debra arranged for at something like $300 an hour. She explained the entire birthing process to the birthmother and again brought out all the instruments. Then Debra had a plethora of questions. I wasn't allowed to join this gathering, but it must have lasted two and a half hours. I think the birthmother finally said *she'd* had enough.

Not yelling at Debra was the hardest part of having the birthmother with us. When she had her mother come out to meet the birthmother I think it actually gave me hemorrhoids from holding in my anger. She had found yet another way to get her family inappropriately involved in a personal situation. I was scared that the two of them with that laugh were going to give the birthmother a miscarriage. Why was my mother-in-law there? Debra wasn't the one who was pregnant!

After five weeks Debra's anxiety was at the most heightened level I had ever witnessed. She wanted that baby immediately, if she had to reach into the birthmother and pull it out herself. I had finally moved the birthmother into a bed and breakfast around the corner. I knew Debra felt she was losing control, but I couldn't take it anymore.

On two occasions Debra's mind went into labor so she subconsciously convinced the birthmother she was in labor and about to have the baby. I had to pick up the birthmother and rush her to the hospital in spite of the fact she was not having contractions. One time it was indigestion and the other she just had to fart. And in my unfeeling way I made fun of Debra's projected feelings by faking my own labor in bed that night and demanding a mid-wife. As usual, I went too far and underestimated just how on edge she was about this whole thing. She wasn't amused.

However, after the gas leak I refused to get up and take anyone to the hospital unless they were crying in pain. And the birthmother would determine that, not Debra. So shortly after the incident, the birthmother woke up, called us and was definitely crying in pain. Debra rolled over and looked at me holding up the phone receiver, "She's crying. Are you satisfied?"

It's really a strange experience when you are about to have a baby that is coming from someone else. You feel really displaced. The birthmother did not want me in the room to see the birth but did want Debra there, so I sat in a waiting room from five in the morning until three in the afternoon just getting updates. I felt like an expectant father in the 1950s. I wished there were a bunch of us in there smoking cigarettes, passing around a flask, calling each other pop and slapping each other on the back telling one another our wife was next. Instead I just sat there for hours and watched coverage of the Columbine Murders on the news, which was the big story of the week.

I was later joined by a couple sets of grandparents who wanted to know why I wasn't in the room with my wife. I spent the entire time explaining who I was over and over and it was really bothering me. Debra was in the birthing room and coming out to give me regular reports, but I wasn't part of the process. I thought maybe I should be in a bar somewhere and just waiting for a phone call to come back.

Often my thoughts drifted as to why I was doing this adoption. It was costing me $10,000, the birthmother could change her mind at any minute and Debra was missing out on the chance to be pregnant, which I know she desperately wanted to experience. But I kept reminding myself I was helping a child who needed caring parents and I was saving one from a life of possible mental illness and visual impairment.

However, the reality of it all was just overwhelming. I was adopting, which is what I believed was right, but it was not as easy to actually do as it is to prophesize about it in a bar half-drunk. And I wondered how I was going to feel when a nurse put someone else's child in my arms and said, "This is yours." Would I talk the talk and walk the walk and say, "Yes, this is mine. It doesn't matter one bit whose womb it came from"?

Around 3:00 P.M. the birth started happening and I was allowed to sit outside the room and actually hear what was going on, but only Debra was allowed inside where all the action was. I actually heard a lot of women giving birth and screaming in pain and felt like I wanted to pass out. It was excruciating to hear it all. I didn't know which scream was coming from the birthmother and which was from some other woman. All I knew was a lot of vaginas were being torn apart and somewhere there was a guy worrying if things would ever be the same.

Finally, a nurse called me in. The first thing I saw was a bloody placenta sliding around in a steel dish on a table and I almost hit the floor. It was quite unnerving. I had to look away. But then I saw Debra smiling at me. The birthmother was looking the other way. And to my amazement a nurse handed me a baby girl. I couldn't believe it. They gave her right to me. I was the first to hold her. It was one of the most selfless and meaningful things Debra ever did for me. She knew I needed that and wanted me to have it. Debra always got the big things right.

That baby girl was so beautiful that I could feel my eyes well up with tears and after that I never once questioned whose daughter she was.

She was ours. I got to cut the remainder of her umbilical cord, they wrapped her up like a super-burrito and I sat down with her on a couch and held her for what seemed like hours. I just stared at her. I could see her personality then as it is today with each of her gestures and vocalizations. I now believe we are born with a particular temperament. It's just that people don't always realize it until the child gets older.

It was the best day of my life. Obviously, because I now was the proud father of a beautiful baby girl. But also because I knew for once I did the right thing. I proved I wasn't all talk. Oh, I knew that one day she'd want to know about her biological mother and father and all the emotional issues that would rise. However, I just didn't care. I loved Debra for letting me do the right thing. Like I said, she always got the big things right.

As for all of you fellow bipolars who decided to have biological children; it's your choice. I am not better than you. I just did what I thought what was right. And it was the one thing I did in my life of which I am not ashamed.

The Walk of Shame

Mrs. Barber did not take any shit. She wanted your homework on time, done right and for you to be able to speak in class intelligently about what you'd been studying. Everything I could not do. She also demanded you to read the newspaper and discuss current events. And if you couldn't spell a word you looked it up in the dictionary. She expected a lot from her third graders.

But I was the class clown. I was always depressed and felt like nobody liked me. I thought I was a loser and couldn't do the work. So I hoped that by making people laugh it would make me popular and happy. What I didn't realize was that usually people were laughing at the class clown, not with him. And Mrs. Barber didn't tolerate clowns in her classroom. Needless to say, I spent a lot of time out of the classroom. On occasion she physically threw me out.

So, the day of the big church service (it was a Christian school) I could not stand on the balcony, the plateau every student in that lower-middle school wanted to reach, and sing songs to the baby Jesus with my class. I had to make the lonely, humiliating Walk of Shame down to the second grade classroom. I sat with them showing the sullen face of an Indian Chief until I had to take a far greater Walk of Shame into the chapel and sit with the second grade class, where *everyone* knew I was in third grade and wondered what I had done. The snickering was unbearable.

I detested being at a faith-based school. Of course it was again one of my mother's ideas. Since I have had nystagmus since birth causing poor eyesight, even with glasses, she felt I needed to be seated close to the blackboard. In her mind that could only happen in a private school with smaller classes. A public school could not possibly allow me to sit up front. And the best private school in the area was Christian faith-based. However, I spent most of my time there standing in the hallway being punished. Sitting near the blackboard was a moot point. And I could have done this in public school for a lot less money.

And of course my father agreed, so my maternal grandparents footed the bill. And every time they visited the school my grandfather would "take the headmaster aside" and remind him of that. He didn't want my dad to accidentally get a "thank you note" in the mail.

The first private school Walk of Shame came in first grade on the first day before our first church service. It was my first church service, as well. I was also wearing a tie and sport coat for the first time. The tie was plaid and the sport coat was blue, made out of a fabric resembling the upholstery of a 1972 Cadillac DeVille. It had a difficult-to-see pattern, but you could feel it if you ran your fingers over it.

Before services began the headmaster summoned me to his office. Right away I thought I had done something wrong. I couldn't imagine why he could possibly want to see me. My mind was going a mile a minute when I walked in and his church-lady secretary sat me down on an uncomfortable chair in his office that looked like Quakers built it. Finally the headmaster walked in wearing one of Richard Nixon's grey suits with freshly Brill Creamed hair and sat down next to me. Was my tie tied wrong? Was I rude to someone? Did I break a rule?

He put a kind hand on my shaking hand clutching the chair's armrest. He smiled, "Peter, I just want you to know you are no different from anyone else here."

I must have had the most utterly blank look on my face. Was he going to tell me that I really was retarded but at this school they were going to treat me like a normal kid? I remained silent.

"I mean the fact that you are Jewish and nobody else here is. It's perfectly okay. You are no different from anyone else. You do not need to feel uncomfortable." He gave me a big waxy smile. The Brill Cream in his hair glistened.

Until that very moment I never realized I was different by being Jewish. But now it was top of mind. "Okay. Thank you," was all I could think to say. I thanked the man for allowing me to be Jewish.

"Good, son." And I was released back to my classroom. I took the Walk of Shame from the headmaster's office back to my classroom and came in late in front of everyone. To add to the humiliation, when people asked me why I had to go see the headmaster all I could think to say was, "Because I'm Jewish." I was mortified.

I almost wished he confirmed my fears about being retarded and not comprehending it. Living in comatose oblivion seemed better than this. I knew nothing about my religion except that I hated going to synagogue, my parents faked piousness and I wasn't so sure I believed in God. And now *I* was representing the entire Jewish religion in my school with grades one through eight.

And let me tell you, in that little town of Bethlehem there were a lot of parents who did not want their children playing with a Jew. It's hard when your best friend in fourth grade is told by his mother he is not allowed to play with you anymore because you're Jewish.

Unfortunately Mrs. Barber was Jewish. And in addition to making sure I was completely literate and a citizen of the world, she also called on me to explain every Jewish holiday each time one of those little bastards reared its ugly head. The ultimate prepubescent Walk of Shame was up to the front of her sixth grade classroom to light the menorah for the first day of Hanukah. Yes, I drew the short straw and had her again in sixth grade. Little did I know my meddling mother had put in the fix because she felt Mrs. Barber was "good for me." Looking back it's one of the few things she did right.

Anyway, I could not light the match. I was afraid of burning myself. And the more she ridiculed me the more nervous I got and eventually started to cry. I was afraid of lighting matches. Finally she lit the match and I took the tearful Walk of Shame back to my desk. You'd think most teachers would be glad I didn't like lighting things on fire. Not Mrs. Barber.

Well, I think she'd be very pleased to know I practiced very hard at lighting matches. Eventually I learned to light cigarettes, joints, pipes, bongs, firecrackers, M-80's and black gunpowder, too. Oh, and of course Hanukah candles.

Mrs. Barber humiliated me more times than I can remember. I mastered the Walk of Shame under her tutelage. But I have to say, the things I learned from her about reading and writing, social etiquette, verbal skills, keeping up with current events, attention to detail and learning to use resources around me were the most important things I ever had ingrained into my mind. She taught the old-fashioned way, and rammed what I needed to know down my throat in spite of what was going on in my head. It's much appreciated. I might not have absorbed it any other way. No pain, no gain.

But the Walks of Shame continued. When you're bipolar II and sometimes suffer from hypomanic episodes, you are bound to embarrass yourself in ways you cannot even begin to imagine. One minute you're up, the next minute you're down. And you have no control over the severity of each wave of emotion. It's like you're in the ocean and being pulled by the undertow. You can't fight it so you have to go with it. It might suck you under or make you ride high on a big beautiful wave. But you don't get to decide.

Let's jump to a neighborhood tussle when I couldn't have been more than nine years old. Some kids across the street were picking these hard berries from trees and throwing them at my brother, Andy, and me on our front lawn. So, solemn warriors that we were, we started collecting the berries, too, plus other random items like tin cans and rocks, wailing these items back at them. But nobody was connecting with any good shots on either side.

Then a seven-year-old mercenary girl from the other side, spawned from the white-trashiest family on the street, ran onto our lawn for a close shot at me. Being that she was a younger girl and completely unwashed, I just pushed her away. And to Andy's and my amazement, she did three cartwheels, a summersault, spun around twice, slid across the street on her stomach and slammed into the curb teeth first. We were stunned. She ran home bleeding, leaving a trail of un-brushed teeth.

Andy and I ran in our house and realized nobody was going to believe that I barely touched her. I was in trouble. My mind was going a mile a minute. I needed to be hurt, too, so we taped my right eye up with about five Band-Aids and went back outside. The story would be that the little miscreant caused serious damage to my eye with a rock and I might never recover. Of course when my mother saw my brother's patchwork we had to come clean. You just can't tell your mother you almost lost your eye in a fight but not to worry, thanks to your little brother it's under control with Band-Aids.

Four hours later, when the neighbor girl came home from the hospital, my mother made me take the Walk of Shame across the street to apologize to her and see if there was anything I could do. I felt this was so unfair because I did not do anything to warrant such consequences. Yet here I was being held accountable. I was powerless over my depression and now things in real life were working against me. This brought a feeling I would become all too familiar with in later life: hopelessness. It wasn't fair and I think it was the first time I actually thought of wanting to commit suicide, although not in so many words. I was on the precipice of feeling like life was against me no matter what I did.

So I apologized to the fat mom with the bra straps hanging out of her halter top and belly over her jeans, her live-in boyfriend with his hair in his eyes, zits around the corners of his mouth and nose, and alas her now-front-toothless, acrobatic daughter. She had stitches on both knees and both elbows wrapped in bandages. Fortunately, the lost teeth were baby teeth. I made a solemn apology and then I cried – half out of embarrassment and half out of the injustice of it all. My mother just stood there the whole time and looked the other way. Nobody cared that the girl was an acrobat.

To my mother, these people were beneath her, and she didn't even want to talk to them. After all, she didn't push anyone. And she didn't want to entertain the idea that I might be telling the truth. So I would pay the price. She would teach me a lesson. But all she was doing was delivering me to the white trash family's doorstep. She started walking away when I was still standing there bawling. When I saw her go I ran to her and she said I embarrassed her and to go away. I guess you could say

I had a double header Walk of Shame that day – to the acrobat's house and away from my embarrassed mother.

As I got older my Walks of Shame increased. I wanted to fit in and I didn't. And since I was either depressed or manic, I would tend to do or say things that were out of the norm and would often cause me grave embarrassment. But I couldn't stop. At forty-five I am just learning how to avoid these situations.

In junior high school, eighth grade in particular, it must have seemed to people that I had no shame. My parents had separated and I was living in Philadelphia with my manic mother and normal brother. I was attending a public school for the first time in my life. And for the first time ever girls were finding me attractive. Frankly, I couldn't believe it. I thought I was one of the ugliest kids on earth; my hair would never stay feathered properly, as was the style in 1979. It was a constant battle against zits to keep me from turning me into Elephant Boy and the slightest activity would cause me to perspire like an overweight stockbroker going nuts on the trading floor. Sweating made my hair go curly in the front like a drainage ditch and my heavy glasses to slip off my nose. To top it off, I was clumsy and nervous in new situations.

Public middle school in Philadelphia was completely different from private school in a small town. There were all types of kids from all walks of life: rich, poor, kids from working class families and kids from parents who were doctors and lawyers. And a lot of Jewish kids and teachers, too. It was like a huge Sunday brunch buffet and I had no idea what I should be eating first: eggs, pancakes, fruit, cereal, steak or seafood. There were so many types of kids with which to engage. To top it off, I kept hearing that girls thought I was cute. At first I thought kids were just making fun of me, but when boys started telling me I was a "lucky dog," I started to believe it wasn't a dream. I also had no idea what to do about any of this except go home and jerk off every afternoon thinking about the possibility I might actually get laid.

Unfortunately, I blew apart what could have been the chance to be popular and normal by acting like a heat-seeking missile and attaching myself to the group everyone called the "burnouts." They were a bunch of kids who smoked cigarettes and pot, were always in search of harder drugs, breaking into houses and cars and stealing from the school store.

We were basically little assholes aspiring to be petty criminals. We were always fighting someone, trying to con someone into something or beating on one another. We took pride in the fact all the other cliques, especially the jocks, hated our guts.

So here I was with a chance not to be a loser for once in my life. Nobody ever gets a chance like this. And I doubted and hated myself so much I made sure I riddled that self with bullets and then ran it over twice with a tractor trailer, just to make absolutely sure it was dead and could never, ever be resurrected.

So once I was officially categorized as a burnout, my options became limited. None of the really nice girls wanted anything to do with me. So in my thirteen-year-old brilliant mind, I decided I would make everyone notice me. I resumed my profession of class clown, picked fights with kids I knew I could beat, embarrassed girls, stole money from the school store cigar box, cut class, hid out, smoked on campus and made a pot pipe in shop class.

Every day I was shaming myself by trying to be the ultimate badass. And I was so public about it that even my fellow burnout buddies didn't want me around. I was actually embarrassing a gang of kids who shook down younger kids for their lunch money and taunted kids in special education classes. During the last three months of classes every day of school was a Walk of Shame. What killed me about this was that I had done it to myself. I was like a maniac destroying my life and I couldn't stop it. I was acting out at a fevered pitch, saw myself doing the wrong thing, heard people telling me I was hurting myself – but the train had left the station and I couldn't stop it.

Of course it didn't help that my mother was acting like a maniac on the home front. And when she started hearing from the school about my out-of-control behavior and her screaming and hitting me wasn't an effective deterrent, she sent me to a psychiatrist.

My psychiatrist suspected something chemical was taking place. He put me on Mellaril to initially calm me down when I was at the vortex of almost being kicked out of school. I don't remember how long I took it, but it did make a difference. I just recall panicking when I had a self-induced orgasm and nothing came out. I thought it was permanent and became scared out of my mind. When your penis malfunctions at fourteen it's worse than getting brain cancer.

I frantically tried to contact an older guy in my apartment building to talk me down, which would have been completely inappropriate and made for countless Walks of Shame. Thank god he wasn't home. Still, I needed an answer immediately or I thought I would kill myself as I stumbled down the ladder of manliness. Finally I got a hold of my dad. This was good because I was almost prepared to go out on the street, get on a city bus and ask the driver what could have caused this situation. I was beside myself with thoughts of sexual dysfunction. But my fears of permanent "ghost orgasms" were finally assuaged when my dad told me it had to be the Mellaril. Of course, the medication! I threw the bottle in the dumpster in the parking lot so it could never end up in our medicine cabinet again. Sperm killer!

Well, things were bad at home with my mother and her new high-wasted boyfriend. I was a huge disciplinary problem in school. My dad lived in a tiny apartment about fifty miles away and did not relish losing his freedom by taking me in. I also got caught cutting school in my friend Brenda's apartment and my psychiatrist felt I should be put in foster care. Inside I was depressed and manic both at the same time although I couldn't verbalize it, nor could it even be diagnosed in 1980 as actually a mixed state. I was hyper and exhausted all at the same time, yet I couldn't stop acting like a human lighting rod. It was being forced to live two severe emotions at once. All I could do was pray for unconsciousness, which was the only thing that could make it stop. Worst of all, I was still undiagnosed as bipolar, so I had no idea what was happening to me.

Finally my dad agreed to take me in and I was relegated to living with him in Bethlehem, Pennsylvania, and going back to the private school where I had spent most of my life. That was going to be a major Walk of Shame, as I had walked out of there the year before for a city public school and made it clear I never wanted to look back. And I would be stuck in Bethlehem with my dad actually having to be a parent, where I'd learn it would not be easy on me. Furthermore, only getting into the city every other weekend to visit my mother always ended badly with a knock-down, drag-out mother-son fight. And the mixed states had morphed into good-old-fashioned deep depression as I began my four-year ordeal of high school in the little town of Bethlehem. Now I was just plain suicidal.

I can't tell you which part was worse, going to a school where I had no friends and a reputation for being an asshole, or coming home every night to have my day deconstructed by my father in his underwear, handkerchief tucked in the waistband ready to throw like a football penalty flag while sitting at the dinner table and hearing something he didn't like. We ate frozen dinners he baked in a toaster oven and between criticisms I'd hear solemn suction noises from his firmly closed mouth, securely chewing his cud amidst heavy nostril breathing. Then I'd spend the rest of my night sitting in my room staring at the homework I had no patience to do and daydreaming about a life away from there, contemplating whether it would really ever happen. Eventually my dad would yell from the other room that it was time to go to bed. In the morning the whole thing started all over again.

The only break I'd get was when I'd come home from school and my dad wasn't home yet to start lecturing me about my grades or a call he got from a teacher because I was acting out in class. He also wanted me to join a Jewish social group to make more friends; just the thought of it turned my stomach. I hated religion. It made me feel stupid about things that weren't even real.

My dad was constantly trying to whip me *back into shape* like eventually my spine would crack and I'd say, "Wow, I think I'm better. I am going to join the lacrosse team at school and talk to the rabbi about getting Bar Mitzvahed again. Hey, I wonder if he has any daughters? Whoa, it's eight o'clock and I haven't started my studies yet. I'll never get in to your old law school at this rate!" Music to his ears.

I'd usually come home from school and spend those precious hours of alone time contemplating how to kill myself. Sometimes I'd call to chat for a bit on the suicide hotline. Other times I'd just hold the kitchen knife to my wrist too scared to make the incision. Or, I'd just jerk off to one of my father's *Playboys* (he'd saved every edition since the early seventies) and then smoke cigarettes until he came home.

The depression magically lifted in tenth grade. It was as if someone pulled the wet blanket off my head. I stopped being the class clown, kept to myself, made an effort to do my schoolwork and joined the wrestling team. Through the wrestling team and not being such a jerk, I made some friends. And I was so happy to have kids who liked me I ended up befriending all types of people. The problem was, none of them liked each other. So, I hung out with different friends for different reasons. But nobody got along so we could never all hang out together.

And each friend was always asking, "Why are you hanging around with this or that asshole?"

I wanted to say, "Because they like me. It's been a long dry spell with no friends." But instead I'd just say, "Oh, he's ok. You just have to get to know him. He's got great taste in music," or something to that effect.

But still my self-confidence was in the shitter. Case in point was my forte for dating ugly girls. I didn't think I was capable of getting an attractive girlfriend, so I'd always go for the one who liked me no matter what model Buick she resembled. I dated this one girl who went to a different school. I actually didn't ask her out, she asked me out. And I said yes because I thought she was the best I could do. I even convinced myself she wasn't that bad. But the few times we went out I had this uncomfortable sensation that she looked like a guy in school I knew named Chris Waxman. It was really starting to bother me. But I put it out of my head.

Well, finally it was time for one of my friends to meet her. I got tickets to a David Bowie concert at the Spectrum in Philadelphia. My girlfriend was bringing a date for my friend and the four of us were going together.

When I introduced him to the two girls he didn't say much. I was beginning to think my girlfriend was not as bad as I thought. Who cares if her shoulders were like a football player's and she looked as if she was always about to sneeze? Then as I was driving everyone to the concert my friend leaned over to me and exclaimed, "I got it!"

"Got what?" I enquired.

"Chris Waxman. Your girlfriend looks like Chris Waxman!" He burst out laughing.

Now that he'd said it I had to face it. She did look like Chris Waxman. I had to break it off. I could never kiss her again without thinking I was making out with Chris Waxman, this total Dead Head in school with whom I wrestled. And for the rest of the evening my friend just looked at me sitting with her and snickered. It was an entire Evening of Shame.

When word got out in school it was weeks of Walking in Shame. All because I didn't think I was worthy of getting a girl that I would have liked to date and took the first one that showed any interest in me, whether I was interested or not. This would be a repeating theme in my social life. Dwarfs, midgets, fat women, sloppy women, retarded women, crazy women – I dated them all. I feared my wedding would begin with the ultimate Walk of Shame. Right down the aisle with one of these beasts of burden.

The Mood Stabilizer Blues

Mood stabilizers. The doctors tell you that when you're manic depressive these are the most important pieces to the consortium of pills you have to swallow. They keep antidepressants from taking you too high and the tranquilizers from taking you too low. The problem is they make you feel completely apathetic toward everything life has to offer.

Nothing is exciting and nothing is devastating. You just exist in this middle ground, the DMZ (Demilitarized Zone) of bipolar illness. You can see all the shooting on either side, but you can't go there. You have to just sit and live life in this altered no-frills state of plain old existence.

In 1999 my wife and I were taking a group of my clients for a ten-day cruise to the Tahitian Islands. All expenses were paid by the television station I worked for and my instructions were, "Don't let anyone pay for anything. The station will reimburse you." And, this was the most opulent cruise you could imagine. We even took a limo to the airport and hosted a pre-trip cocktail party.

Debra was out of her mind with excitement. She understood what an opportunity this was for us. It was a payoff for all my hard work to be able to host my clients on such a colossal trip. But even the day of the flight I couldn't muster up a chill of excitement in my stomach. The whole thing felt like a pain in the ass and I'd be just as happy staying home and watching *Cops* on television, picking my nose and adding to the booger farm I had been cultivating on back of the headboard to our bed. I was depressed about the thought of dragging suitcases halfway around the world and taking a marathon flight to get there. And, I had to be on my best behavior for ten days without a manic outburst giving anyone a hint I was mentally unbalanced. Internally, I was numb about the whole thing. That is what a mood stabilizer can do to you. Take the trip of a lifetime and equate it with picking your nose.

So, while on mood stabilizers I had to find a way to artificially pump myself up. Otherwise I would positively die of existing in a state of utter numbness. And sex was the first thing that came to mind. My wife and I were having none of it. She had a low sex drive and consequently wasn't putting out a whole hell of a lot of pheromones. What she did emit might as well have been Lysol.

Sex was something I wanted more of, but not from my marriage. Somewhere along the line I had lost the lust for Debra. She was still an attractive woman, but I had no passion. And, I was relatively sure it wasn't coming back. However, I thought I could handle staying married if I found sexual stimulation outside of the home. But I wasn't interested in going to a prostitute. At least, not consciously.

It began with me going online and scheduling massages. I was looking for the legit kind at first, but I had to have a great-looking female masseuse. In the back of my mind I was always hoping something more would happen. Like maybe the masseuse would mistake my penis for my arm and keep shaking my hand until I ejaculated.

So, I'd get all excited about these appointments. I'd get a massage once a week always by someone different, trying to "strike gold." For seven days I'd ruminate on my upcoming session and who would be massaging me. Then I'd lie on my big erection atop some massage table on a Friday after work and get an $80 massage praying the therapist would say, "I don't normally do this, but you look like you could use a release and I really don't mind doing it. It's really just a massage when you think about it, just on your penis."

Then I'd roll over, she'd be standing there in her panties, grab my meager shaft and I'd explode like a champagne bottle. I would obsess about this scenario the entire week before I met each therapist. It kept

128

life a little interesting. But the event never happened. Why did everyone have to be such a professional?

But these "strictly professional" dick teasers were not doing the trick and I was quickly slipping back under the wet blanket of mood stabilization. I found I could slosh my way out if I went to some of the porn sites and Craigslist where the "Happy Ending Queens" advertised their therapeutic skills. I figured it was time to stop bullshitting around, and as soon as I started making some inquiries my heart started beating again.

The first wrist flicker I selected was because we had the same last name, so I trusted her. The stupidity behind that reasoning was immeasurable. But I was so worried about getting caught I thought that if she was a Goodman, too, it might help in my defense. Like, "Debra, I thought she was a relative and that's why I was over at her apartment." Or, "She tricked me. She said we were related so of course I thought it was going to be a normal massage. Do you think I'd fool around with a relative?"

Naturally, we weren't related. She also wasn't a complete beauty. But she gave a great massage. Then she rolled me over and I heard her slip on elastic gloves like she was going to do the dishes. But she did it so fast and effortlessly I knew she was a pro. Then she engulfed my organ with a ton of lubricant and I sprayed all over the place like a fire extinguisher in less than a minute.

I thanked her and went home to my wife and daughter where dinner was waiting. And, to my surprise, I learned I was able to handle the guilt. This was unfortunate, because my marital sex life needed help and this whole wide wonderful world of paid hand jobs I'd discovered pretty much eliminated the need to make any effort to fix it.

However, as many massages and end caps I received, I never did cross the intercourse line. I could rationalize a *strong finish* to a massage, but not sex. But the thought of it *accidentally* happening during a session added to my excitement level. "What if she slipped it in before I could say anything?" I would wonder. "That surely could not be my fault," conveniently ignoring the fact that I was in a massage parlor on my own volition. There would be no accidents.

But after a while it got a little old. I wanted a girlfriend and couldn't afford to keep getting knob jobs once a week. My marriage, our boring life, friends, Debra's family and our routine was hell on mood stabilizers.

We'd have friends over for dinner and I could hardly keep from yawning when they talked about what pre-school their kids were getting into. I hated their kids. They were little brats who were going to grow up to be big onion heads like their parents. The boys would graduate to wear Dockers and carry BlackBerrys like their fathers and the girls would use pads until they were married, because their mothers won't want them to lose their virginity to a tampon.

And everyone would talk about their boring professional jobs in banks, law offices or as consultants, and I'd keep waiting for the appropriate time to stretch and say, "Wow, it's late. I have to get up early tomorrow," hoping somebody would take the hint and go home.

I kept waiting for Debra to ask me what I had to do tomorrow when I tried to bow out early. Fortunately she never did because she also was chronically tired and wanted to go to sleep. What would I have said to her? "I'm going to the Love-You-Long-Time-Palace-of-Penis-Pleasure. But don't worry, I'll take the dog." She liked when I took the dog out for the day. She thought the eighty-five-pound Greyhound kept me out of trouble.

I'd become completely apathetic about everything, realizing my life was relegated to plastic get-togethers until I died. We'd have hors d'oeuvre, Debra would make dinner and we'd all sit around at the table and talk about our boring lives for hours. I was rotting from the inside out but nobody knew it because I was on mood stabilizers.

I had one friend who would corner me as soon as his wife and kids were out of the room, and start whispering about all the new porno sites on the web that he'd discovered. His palms were sweating when he'd suggest a "guys night out" and hitting the San Francisco strip club scene, as he did every time we got together. He was a total heavy breather. At strip clubs he always pulled his chair right up to the stage floor and put on his reading glasses to thoroughly examine all the vaginas. The serious look on his face was as if he was studying great literature. This snapshot was worth the entire evening.

Then I discovered the joys of drinking. I had always been a drinker, ever since I first got drunk at age thirteen. But I realized getting drunk Thursday through Sunday nights allowed me to step outside myself. Maybe alcohol is a depressant but it was certainly picking me up. So

130

especially on weekends when we had our little dinner parties, I would drink myself into oblivion.

And for some biochemical reason the psychotropic pills I take and a fast metabolism allow me the luxury of consuming large amounts of liquor. Moreover, I'm usually fairly good at keeping my composure and can often be more congenial when I'm loaded. So, I'd stock the house with beer, wine and sometimes hard liquor for these little gatherings and as soon as everyone arrived I'd start with the drinks. And the more smashed I got, the more I enjoyed the company. They became comical to me.

Eventually drinking in the evenings became an every-night thing. To this day I look forward to some sort of alcoholic libation in the evening. It's just one more thing that takes me out of the mood stabilizer DMZ. So although my doctors then, as now, think it's not the best idea in the world to consume alcohol while taking these medications, my reaction to that is this: "You try and live with this disease and take these pills. If drinking helps and I'm not hurting anyone, I'll keep my *Glen Fiddich,* thank you."

The problem is, I don't drink during the day. Plus, alcohol usually makes me a little depressed the day after. Depression in a mood-stabilized state is awful. You feel yourself constantly dropping into the pit and getting a bitter taste of severe suicidal depression. Then the mood stabilizer brings you back up to status quo but you can't forget the memory of the pits of hell you were just treated to a glimpse of. So I found my thrills in jewelry stores and online jewelry sites, buying Swiss watches during the day to lift me up. And I took my brother down with me on this one. Or he took me down; I can't remember who started it.

We always loved watches and my brother and I became obsessed when some of the bigger-faced ones made their debut with complicated automatic Swiss movements. When we weren't on the phone long-distance discussing our next purchases, we were emailing "wrist shots" of our latest acquisitions. I couldn't stand a week to go buy when I wasn't buying or expecting the arrival of a new timepiece. I felt like an expectant father, always pacing in front of my mailbox waiting for the UPS truck to give birth.

And we are talking about watches $2,500 and above. I was buying on credit, getting special financing, raiding other accounts and selling some inventory just to keep the new inventory flowing in. I only lusted after expensive watches. I literally couldn't stop. But it made me so happy. However, as soon as I put a new one on my wrist, I was ready for another conquest.

The emails between my brother and me got cryptic after a year into this thing. For instance, he'd write, "Black Armani shirt, Gray pleated slacks, Bruno Maglia shoes, $200 black leather belt and Omega Planet Ocean [wristwatch]." I'd email back, "Tight combo." Then I'd tell him what outfit I had on and with which watch.

And in my lust to get a brand new timepiece on my wrist, I'd often attempt to size it myself. It could take me hours of heavy breathing and cursing to get the pins and links to cooperate, often damaging the band in the process. But it didn't matter; not only did I have to have the watch, it had to be on my wrist pronto.

I knew my brother was the same way. He told me one time he tried to take a scratch out of a rather expensive watch with a jeweler's resurfacing kit and he ended up changing the finish on the entire watch. Convincing himself that this was a good thing took days.

Unlike me, Andy had no problem parting with his watches to raise cash and make room for new inventory. I've seen things go from jewelry case, to his arm and onto eBay in a matter of hours. Or, he'd go to a department store, purchase a watch, wear it for the weekend and then return it when he grew tired of it. He called this his "timepiece rental program." Only it was better than renting because he never actually had to pay for the watch. He'd just "borrow it for a while."

Well, watches are wonderful. But sometimes my mood stabilizers needed a really big kick in the ass. Something that could bring me pleasure for at least six months. So, in two years I bought five brand new and two classic cars. Sequentially, not all at once. When it came to cars, I was a serial motor-head.

Each car I would purchase would be the ultimate. *The* car I have always wanted. Usually a little extreme, like the Shelby GT 500 Mustang with a 500-horsepower engine; it really belonged on a racetrack.

When I was forty-two, my brother and a friend came to visit and rode in one of my Mustangs. When I cranked up the engine it snarled loud enough to penetrate the interior. Andy then turned around and said to my friend John in the backseat, "This is the car you always wanted in high school but could never have."

I started feeling really stupid until my friend said, "I don't know, I think Pete is kind of like Steve McQueen." I instantly felt better because living in San Francisco and owning a Mustang was my tribute to Steve McQueen, one of my favorite all-time actors. The entire weekend I felt obliged to jump the car over the hills and slide around corners just to reinforce to my brother I was like Steve McQueen with my Mustang in the 1968 movie *Bullet*, not some middle-aged divorced guy coping with midlife crisis by driving the car he always wished for in high school.

However, after six to eight months of owning my "dream car" I'd start to look around and eventually fancy something new. Then the discontentment would start. I would begin to invent issues why this particular car wasn't right for me. Or why I needed a newer model.

Eventually I'd start looking at new cars online just for fun. Then one day it would turn into an obsession and fill me with consternation and excitement simultaneously. I knew I was about to make a costly mistake but I couldn't stop the train.

Next, all will power would break down. I'd leave the office on a fabricated sales call and swing by the dealer to trade in my not-even-one-year-old car for a new one. I didn't care about the penalties or how much I'd have to put down, just as long it was reasonable and I could handle the payments. I barely even paid attention to the finance guy. I just wanted the new car. I needed the lift. No research. No comparison-shopping. No nothing. I decided what I wanted, pulled into the lot with my "old" new car and out with my "new" new one. And each car was always a little more insane in some aspect than the last.

But with the new car would come a Walk of Shame and period of depression. The Walk of Shame was driving into the parking garage at my non-profit place of employment and having to explain why I had yet another expensive new car. It went against the culture of the place and everyone thought I was wealthy. I'd spend the entire proceeding week disseminating a lie I concocted about why I didn't have to put any money down and it was an even trade, or that my other car was stolen, wrecked, etc. I was extremely embarrassed. The truth was that I "bipolared" it.

And, after a while, I couldn't tell my dad. This is the man who, when I mentioned I had started dating after my divorce, got angry and said it was too expensive for me and I should "cut it out." I was back to lying and hiding things like I was in high school. I was beginning to wonder if my life was going to go full circle at some point. If so I was definitely going to kill myself. No botched suicides. I'd do it right this time.

As if I did not have enough self-inflicted financial pressure with the watches and bi-annual new cars, I was buying 1973 Cadillac Eldorado convertibles from eBay sight unseen. I had always wanted one and my downstairs neighbor was a collector. Finally divorced and with nobody to tell me "no," I bought a rusty one from New York state and had it shipped to San Francisco, pouring in $10,000 getting it roadworthy. I also incurred the joys of paying for storage, registration, insurance and a lot of other little unpleasantries. But I was already in too deep.

However, even after all that the car was far from perfect, so I sold it at a loss and bought another from South Carolina—sight unseen so as not to break my stupid streak—and had it shipped out. A much better vehicle, I still had to put some money into it and bear the brunt of re-registration in California, which is over $700. And for this Eldo I had to take a loan out to purchase. Now I had two car payments! But god-dmanit, I wasn't in the DMZ anymore, I was just stressed out of my mind. I was hemorrhaging money I didn't have from every orifice and I did it all to myself. All because I couldn't stand the living in the no man's land of mood stabilizers. I craved mania. Something to make me feel I was alive. And I also knew I was not going to live forever so why save all the fun stuff for later when I may be too physically sick or whacked out of my head to enjoy it?

I'm the guy who cashes in his IRA at forty-five because he'll have more fun with the money now than when he's in a wheelchair wearing a bib. What can he do with it then, buy a motorized wheel chair?

I imagined emailing my brother Andy from the nursing home: "Plaid bathrobe, blue hospital gown, white plastic bib, green slippers and… blue Tag Heuer Monaco watch…just like Steve McQueen!"

I'm Heavy, He's My Brother

My brother Andy and I have a relationship built on making fun of people. He lives on the east coast and I live on the west coast. And when we talk on the phone, email and get together, we spend the entire time ridiculing family and friends. We don't do it to their faces. It's just between us. So as long as the object of our jokes doesn't know, I don't believe it hurts anyone. Don't let anyone tell you anything different. Kids, it's okay to make fun of anyone if you're discreet.

Andy is also the funniest person I know when it comes to satire. Case in point: my maternal grandfather was such a bad driver that one time he parallel parked about two feet from a curb, and my brother asked if he could call a cab to the sidewalk. I later learned this was a line bastardized from the movie *Annie Hall*. But neither of us had recalled it.

Or another time my grandfather was beeping at a pedestrian nowhere near his car. My brother then aptly pointed out someone getting out of bed in a nearby apartment building window and suggested my grandfather beep at him, too.

Or there was the time Andy and his wife spent a week in England. They came back in a huge fight because Andy insisted on greeting everyone in an overly distorted English accent. He was even calling people "old boy" and asking "if they could please pass the crumpets." My ex-sister-in-law was so embarrassed she would not talk to him for weeks. But as is our way, Andy wouldn't stop.

Andy and I are actually thinking of going to England so we can have heated public arguments in thick British accents that even the English can't understand. I might even have my right eyebrow surgically raised higher than my left so I can achieve a permanent look of consternation on my face like a true Englishman.

But my nephew is a very perceptive boy. When he started to get older and saw Andy and me spending our time together taking a joke and beating it to death, making fun of people using thick Indian accents for days at a time or recalling again and again how a friend threw up on himself like a fountain at the midnight movies years earlier, he called us on it. Of course Andy explained to him that jokes go through many stages, and if you persist after they stop being funny sooner or later they become funny again, only this time to an even greater degree. At least this has always been our philosophy.

Things weren't always so funny for Andy and me. I remember Andy as a little kid with long blond hair and piercing green eyes in the mid-1970s, being dragged into his room by his arm and smacked around by my mother as she intermittently screamed at him about one incomprehensible thing or another. And Andy would pretty much take it without much of an outburst of emotion, which I'm sure pissed her off even more. She liked to see the pain. Then she'd tell him not to leave his room and slam the door shut.

No matter whether Andy and I were in a fight or getting along, when one of us was getting hit we always felt bad for the other. We were united with the disdain for our parents and their irrational meting out of nonsensical punishment.

I was not as cool about it as Andy. It got to me a lot more as I was very fragile emotionally. All I can remember is that when I was being beaten, I'd call my mom a bitch or some other word I read on the wall in a public restroom, which would make her go even more crazy on me. And when she finally left and slammed my door shut I'd scream for half an hour about how I hated her until she came in and started hitting me again. I just couldn't control my emotions. I couldn't play it cool. I knew something was wrong with either why or how I was being punished.

But because I was a kid I could never be right and would never know for sure until I was older. The frustration of it was overpowering and I couldn't keep it inside. So whenever either of my parents became perplexed or angry and they felt it necessary and appropriate to lay hands on their children, I always made it worse with my emotional outbursts goading them on. My defiance almost justified their abuse. But I couldn't hold in the outburst of anger triggered by their unjust treatment of us. Andy was just better at taking it in stride. I don't think I realized until we were older that he just bottled it up.

This rage that constantly erupted from my dad over things like not rolling up the toilet paper properly, or from my mother if she had had a fight with the cleaning lady, was so ridiculous that the only way to deal with it was for Andy and me to make fun of it. Nobody was ever going to stand up and say, "Hey, these kids are right. Their parents' behavior is deplorable. Let's emancipate them so they never have to deal with this again."

We didn't even know kids could actually be right about something. But we did know we could laugh at our parents' behavior. It certainly was the closest we were ever going to come to any kind of validation that we weren't always at fault. So we began imitating the vacant and crazed look in my mother's eyes when she was hitting us with a hairbrush and trying to sputter words out at the same time. Or, my father chasing us around the house in his underwear screaming to come hither because he was going to give us a "licking." Andy and I thought the word "licking" was something you'd say if you lived in Alabama. Where the fuck did he get that euphemism?

So, that's where I think our snarky humor began. As a coping mechanism that outlived its usefulness. Now it just exists for our pleasure. Or does it?

I imagine being Andy. He stayed on the east coast, close to family. He is the one who has had to deal with sickness, death and probating wills. Plus, over the course of his adult years he must have gotten at least five phone calls from me on the west coast at all hours to say "goodbye." I'd be in the throes of suicide, drunk, taking pills and so completely out of my head that I don't even remember calling. Sometimes he'd have no idea where I was or who on my side of the continent knew what was going on with me. He'd have to track down someone nearby who could intervene and just pray he did it in time. Until recently I never realized what these phone calls did to my brother.

Once when Andy was in Philadelphia on business, he opened the door to his Acura and some idiot driver clipped it clean off his car. That made him so angry he threw up his arms and accidentally knocked over a cup he had just used to take an emergency piss in all over his nice leather interior. It was the conclusion of a very bad week, which he went on to tell me started with one of my suicidal phone calls. It was the first time I stopped to think about what I put him through when I call in such a precarious mental state and how helpless he felt when I did so.

He was literally consumed with worry about me, hence the frequent phone calls he had made to me that week until he felt I was out of the danger zone. And what floored me was that I never realized what I was doing to him. I put myself in his shoes and thought, "My god, if he loves me as much as I love him he must have been a mess." And I know he does, so that is the part killing me.

The other part is that it took me almost nineteen years to realize this. I was extremely selfish not to "get it." What puzzles me is why I wasn't more in tune with his feelings. I guess I always saw Andy as being so strong that I never stopped to understand he is sensitive, too. Ever since the early days of my father chasing us around in his tightie-whities trying to give us the "lickings of our little lives," I just thought he could handle things that usually made me an emotional wreck. But just because he didn't say much didn't mean he didn't feel much.

It was clear for a long time that Andy was miserable in his marriage. His wife over-mothered my niece and nephew to the point where she followed them around the house with air purifiers and talked them to death about every possible concern a seven and eleven-year-old could possibly have. Then she'd upset them with the things they would need to be concerned with in the future.

Andy was a second-class citizen, always in the doghouse for going to the gym or enjoying his watch hobby. The only thing he was good for was supporting everyone in the style to which they had become accustomed. Again, he was carrying a heavy burden.

Eventually the marriage ended. But through it all he was able to look on the lighter side. Even when his soon to be ex-father-in-law accused him of adultery, Andy reminded him of all the times he'd been sighted getting blowjobs in his car in front of a certain drinking establishment, wearing his oversized, gaudy diamond-encrusted pimping glasses. Andy thought the optician was just joking when he showed him the glasses, but his ex-father-in-law actually bought them. That story must be told over and over at optician conferences throughout the world by a bunch of men with glasses adjusting tools and eye measuring sticks in their front shirt pockets.

I'm a pretty heavy guy with my bipolar and OCD. I'm just really glad to have my brother. He is definitely the strong, levelheaded one in the family. I just have to remember not to break his back with my problems. He needs to save some of his humor for his own shit.

Radio Daze

All my life I was fascinated with radio. In the days of AM, I loved tuning in distant stations at night, trying to see from how far away I could pull in a signal through the static and make out the call letters. I could lie in bed all night and do this. I had no idea there was a formal name for the activity called DXing. At the time I didn't understand how amplitude modulation or a skip signal worked, but I was always mesmerized by radio.

When I was really young, I thought the bands actually played music live in a studio. I could never understand how they all got in and out of my local stations so fast and sometimes show up a few times a day. And what were they doing in Pennsylvania all the time? Weren't they supposed to be in L.A.?

I was a music fan at a very early age but in second grade I ended up with a Bobby Sherman lunch box, through no fault of my own. Bobby Sherman was a cheesy Zac Efron-like TV star and bubblegum pop singer. You know, "Easy Come, Easy Go?" That lunchbox only lasted a year, though. The flack I got for it from the boys in school was too much to bear. The only thing worse for my self-image would have been to carry a David Cassidy lunch box.

Actually, my grandparents were the ones who bought it for me. All they knew was I liked music. They had no idea what they were doing. They probably just asked some teenage girl at K-Mart who was cool and she said, "Bobby Sherman." So, they bought me a lunch box with his picture on it. And I was very sensitive about hurting people's feelings, so I made a big deal about loving it. I even convinced myself of it. You have to do that if you are a second-grade boy who takes the bus to school with older kids. If you feel as "gay" as they are going to say you are, it's over. You'll start talking to teachers during recess and covering up every time someone throws a fake punch at you. Pretty soon girls will start kicking you and you're a full-fledged "homo" before you really even know what one is. Personally, I think that girl in K-Mart told my grandparents to get me a Bobby Sherman lunch box just to mess with me.

But I especially liked to listen to music on the radio, and how the smooth-talking disc jockeys presented it. I loved how the jingles flowed into the DJ's voice with plenty of reverb and how they then talked over the record right until the singing started. That's called "hitting the post." And when we went to New York on occasion, I was in heaven listening to the greats who helped define the format known as Boss Radio. Just hearing the WABC jingle would send tingles down my spine. I wanted to be a disc jockey. Well, that and a private investigator. And when I visited Los Angeles and heard the legendary KHJ, it blew my mind. Actually, I wanted to be a DJ *in California.* The station's energy and flow intoxicated me.

But living in Philadelphia, I also developed a taste for talk radio. And although it wasn't my ultimate fantasy, I liked the overnight hosts and how they handled the off-the-wall callers. Some of the hosts had incredible guests and did piercing interviews I wished I could have done. By thirteen I was an avid and well-informed talk radio-fan – probably the only listener under sixty.

Yes, talk radio did have the stigma of a sixty-five-year-old woman sitting in her kitchen in Northeast Philadelphia eating a Danish with coffee, screaming at the host's crackly voice coming out of her portable Motorola. She was sure the Russians were amassing at the New Jersey border getting ready to attack and make Popov Vodka the official national drink. I thrived on these nuts calling in. That's what kept it interesting.

So there I was in college, taking my Elavil for my diagnosis of depression and I tried to get a job at the campus radio station. My major was

Radio, Television and Film and as a junior it was about time I got my feet wet. But Temple University had such a renowned program that their radio station was basically professional quality and my chances of getting on the air and doing anything but changing the water cooler tanks were next to nothing. So I took things into my own hands and sought out the lowest-rated station in Philadelphia and applied for an internship.

The station was WDVT Talk 900 AM and I think they were so shocked I wanted to work there just for the experience that they didn't know what to do with me. But in no time I went from stuffing envelopes to engineering live talk programs, producing program content and writing and producing commercials and station promos. I even gave the "Heterosexual Report" on their groundbreaking "Gay Talk" program – at least, groundbreaking for Philadelphia in the 1980s.

This little AM talker made a lot of noise. We had a guest die in the waiting room, during the holidays I once accidentally let a MAMBLA chorus of young boys with their perverted escorts come in off the street to carol on the air, I used to turn on the station too early in the morning and get angry phone calls from the Canadian station I was interfering with, and the parade of celebrities that graced our airwaves was impressive.

But, as most things in my life, my radio dream was killed when the station was sold back to its original parent FM station, practically overnight becoming a classical simulcast with its FM counterpart. And when I graduated college a few months later, the owner of the now silent talk station, who was a Philadelphia Talk Radio legend, told me to go into sales, where the money was. So a frustrated me started a twenty-two-year career of selling airtime. I even ended up at the parent FM classical station that had squelched my talk radio career. It was like going to work for the person who slept with your girlfriend.

Moreover, I really didn't like classical music. God did I try, but even the announcers bothered me. They all spoke like they had snot packed up their noses. To them, classical music was meant to be dry; it was a utility. They took it incredibly seriously and most of them were slightly autistic. They hated salespeople, our flashy clothes and shiny new cars. They felt classical music called for self-imposed suffering. Clearly we were not suffering enough.

By 1994 I had sold for several San Francisco radio stations and each went up for sale during my short tenure. Luckily, I grabbed a lifeboat working for a popular city-regional, four-color glossy magazine and hung on for two years doing quite well. But I missed radio terribly: not selling it, but being on the technical and talent side. Magazines had no cache as far as I was concerned. I was a tower-toothed megahertz man.

So again I searched for the shittiest station in the market and found KATD AM 990, "The KAT," in Concord, California. I immediately landed a Friday overnight air-shift. I wasn't even asked for a demo tape or an audition. Nor was I more than barely trained on the board. I just walked in an hour early for my first shift and the DJ before me showed me how to run it. It was like I was hired to pump gas, so there was no need to show me anything beforehand. I thought, "No wonder they have no ratings." That and the fact that the signal was so weak you couldn't toast a piece of bread on the transmitter.

The shift was from midnight to 7:00 A.M. Most people would be exhausted working all day and then driving an hour to be on air all night, but I loved it. I didn't care if anyone was listening. I experimented with my style and fine-tuned my technical skills. I looked forward to the show every week for an entire year and I put together a decent demo tape. But the long overnight hours took their toll.

Usually I'd be all hyped up on coffee until around 3:00 A.M. I sounded decent and my reflexes were on queue. After three I started to get tired. I'd slur my words, forget to load the next song, hit the wrong buttons and anything else I could do to make the station sound like it was being run by dogs.

By five I didn't even want to talk to anyone, which is a problem if you're a DJ. I'd load up the compact disc machines and set an alarm for two-minute intervals so I could sleep between launching the next song. I'd also start to hallucinate that someone was standing behind me in the studio and would jump out of my chair and let out a little "yelp" now and then, like I had some sort of psychosis. I was dead tired.

After a year the lack of sleep was making me very depressed on Saturdays. By then I was diagnosed as bipolar and learning the value of getting good sleep to keep stable. However, I couldn't let it go. I *needed* to be on the air. Being on the KAT made me feel like I was still in the game, even if it was on the outer-most fringes of it. It would take the station becoming all-Portuguese to get me to leave the airwaves.

I doubt it was anything I did. However, I should have seen it coming. The owner was Portuguese. Their big sponsors were Portuguese. Plus, on weekends during the day they had the most awful Portuguese programming. I couldn't understand it, but it was a bunch of ladies in babushkas all fighting for the microphone playing records that sounded like someone put music to pigs being slaughtered. And it seemed like they were talking to people in the audience by calling out certain names, almost expecting an answer.

I was okay with being let go because a year of doing overnights had worn me down. But the Portuguese certainly are a funny people. They don't get much respect from the rest of Europe because they have slightly misshapen heads, so they come to America and buy low-power radio stations to talk to one another. Like a radio station is a big telephone or something.

Once again I was not living my dream and was now working for CBS Radio Group writing copy. The KAT was in the hands of the Portuguese and I was back to announcing songs to myself on my car radio.

Eleven years went by in which my divorce occurred, I went through nine cars, bought a one bedroom condo, got engaged and finally decided I wanted back on the air. Next I had been employed chasing down corporate supporters for public radio and television and this time I targeted a very progressive rock station, just in a smaller market. Nobody in San Francisco would be interested in me until I updated my technical skills and demo CD. Everything was digital now.

After hearing my 1994 demo tape, in 2009 KRSH FM in Sonoma County's Wine Country gave me a tiny time slot on Saturday mornings. Of course, not for pay. But it was a good chance for me to work up a current demo CD and learn to use up-to-date broadcast equipment. Best of all, I got to program my own music. I was in heaven.

And I proceeded to fuck up their entire computer system on my second day on the air. The music and commercials ran off of a computer that I had to physically pause in order to speak by deleting a hash mark. However, I was directed to never, ever delete a number sign. So naturally I did and the pre-recorded show after mine just played the first hour over and over all morning after I signed off. I knew there was a problem but there was no number to call for help and I was alone in the studio, so I slipped out of the station like a Cheshire cat. Then on Monday morning the program director called me at work and almost fired me. I screwed up the one thing *that simply could not happen.* Sponsors were furious and the station had always maintained the show following mine was live, and now the gig was up. I couldn't believe when the program director let me off with just a warning. It was a major faux pas.

From attending my bipolar support group, I realized making a serious mistake at work is why many people who are bipolar choose not to work and go on permanent disability. They either can't or think they can't handle the responsibility and consequences of screwing up. It's just too much pressure. Shit, I was so embarrassed I wanted to quit. It's just that I really liked what I was doing and did not want to walk away from it. I wanted to take another shot at it. I figured if I made another big mistake and got fired, then so be it. But at least I didn't quit.

I wanted so badly to make KRSH FM my everyday job. But at that time I had to be thankful that at least I got to do it at all. Much to my surprise people seemed to like the music I selected. I got lots of calls asking me why I couldn't be on longer and in a better time slot. I just told them to call the program director. The funny thing was, I was just being myself. The positive reaction was completely unexpected. I just hoped the Portuguese didn't move in and buy the station.

So I just kept driving an hour up to Wine Country at 4 AM every Saturday morning to put out on the airwaves the music I'd like to hear from my own personal collection, such as Mott the Hoople, Lou Reed, Little Milton, Quicksilver Messenger Service, Frank Black and the Catholics, Brian Jonestown Massacre, the Pandoras, the Vaselines and Julian Cope, to name a few artists. And the calls kept coming in telling me they liked it. One guy even said I was one of the last true rock and roll DJs. I never had a compliment so flattering. I knew it was untrue, but it felt good.

Whether listeners bombarded the program director with my accolades or not, I'll never know. But nothing ever happened. I don't think Nate had an ear for music. If he did he'd have to go on air and apologize to his listeners. They were pissed. I was programming what they wanted more of. But being low man on the transmitter tower, everything I did or offered to do was ignored.

Nate was program director of four radio stations in the broadcast group. He had a delusion he was programming the station to sound like a cross between National Public Radio and a college station. It was like neither, but that is what he kept purporting every time he got a chance. All he really did was play the same tired Bonnie Rait, Tom Waits and Los Lobos songs over and over, occasionally sticking his head up Lyle Lovett's ass. The promotions were about as creative as a "Two fer' Tuesday" or an "all request lunch." A turkey could do a better job programming that station.

The funny thing about Nate was that he had a radio name. His last name was Campbell but on the air he went by Nate Matthews. It was ridiculous. It's like I am Peter Goodman but when I go on the air I assume the name Peter Pepsi. What is the difference between Campbell and Matthews? Is Campbell too ethnic? Too hard to pronounce? Was he trying to hide his identity? Did he hate soup? Are you only a real radio guy if you change your name?

So for a year I kept waking up at 3:30 A.M. every Saturday for the hour drive to Santa Rosa. And I'm sure I drove like a drunken sailor trying not to fall asleep, drifting lanes and attempting to maintain a speed that wouldn't land me in jail.

My medications also made my mouth dry and I had trouble not slurring my words on the air. Sometimes I got a little confused. Now and then I couldn't remember the list of songs I just played because the mood stabilizer Topamax, which many call Dope-amax, occasionally leaves my short-term memory dangling. But I loved doing it. I found ways to power through all the obstacles: drink a lot of coffee, drive with the windows down to stay awake, label buttons on the control board NOT to push and laugh at my mistakes on the air. I even made them part of the show. I told my audience I was going to put together a "Best of" CD for all my greatest on-air mistakes. Like the time I made fun of Toyota's "sticky accelerator" safety debacle and then learned I had to promote a remote the station was doing from a Toyota dealer in Petaluma later that day. I had jokingly said on air earlier "that Toyotas were driving themselves off dealer lots so hurry up and catch one!"

Between my bipolar drug side effects of dry mouth, blurred vision and shaky hands, and my poor eyesight which caused me to have everything I had to read on air right in front of my face so I couldn't see the control board, I was probably a sorry-ass excuse for a disc jockey. But I stumbled through and kept trying to improve. I guess my ultimate goal was feeling like I did a job well done, even if nobody was listening or really cared. Nobody would ever truly know what I had to overcome just to be an okay disc jockey while working through all of the side effects of my medications to counteract my illness.

I left "the KRUSH" in the beginning of 2011. Nate Campbell-Matthews, in his infamous wisdom, wanted me to take my successful format and taint it with six of his ass-picks per hour, which would bear out to be half my show. This was the first time he showed interest in anything I did. I knew my listeners would think I sold out, so I figured it was better to keep my dignity and quit. Hold my head high. Don't be anyone's bitch. Never back up from the door. But man do I miss it. I lived for Saturday mornings.

So I continue with my love for music and soliciting radio stations to put me on the air with my demo CD. I always feel so complete when I am behind the microphone. It doesn't matter if my eyes shift, my hands shake or I'm having a bad hair day. Just as long as I have a big cup of coffee and some good music to play, I'm living the dream.

Marathon Man

I sucked at sports. Nor did I have any interest in them. My dad would pitch me a baseball in the front yard and I'd duck because I was afraid of getting hit. I hated doing this in the front yard for another reason as well: all the neighbors could see how bad I was at baseball. Sometimes I'd have an audience just standing there laughing at me. My dad would even laugh at my wussiness. Then he'd get frustrated at my ineptitude and yell at me and I'd scream back that I didn't even want to play in the first place.

Playing baseball bored the kernels out of me. The neighborhood boys always put me in the outfield where there was only the slightest chance of action. I'd stand out there and daydream while a pop fly would inevitably come right at me. So, I'd run away from it and put my glove over my head so I wouldn't be drilled in the head by the ball. I was always afraid of bending my glasses. I constantly had to have them professionally readjusted so they felt just right on my face. Having a friend bend them back into position was not an acceptable substitute.

Football was no better. I couldn't catch and hold onto the ball if my life depended on it. Nor did I want to, because then someone would try to tackle me. I was not only worried about bending my glasses again, but scratching my watch. I also did not want to get hurt when some runny-nosed kid with a crew cut landed on me. But that was secondary to the watch and glasses. My OCD was in fine working order at ten.

149

Then there was swimming. My mother was convinced my frequent earaches warranted tubes being put in my ears to drain trapped water in my ear canals causing the pain, which was a common practice in those days. Wearing earplugs in the pool to keep water out so the tubes would stay in, was the solution for swimming. But my mother insisted I additionally bandage each ear with white plastic medical tape and then wear a bathing cap for extra protection from water seepage. It was emasculating for an 8-year-old boy to suffer through such humiliation for four years. That's why I grew to like the winter better than summer. The summer meant a season of indignity.

So even though I was a good swimmer, I never wanted to go swimming because I was sick of being asked questions like, "Are you a boy or a girl?" or, "Where is the top part of your bathing suit, young lady?" Plus I couldn't hear anything. And if I took the cap off it looked like I'd had ear surgery the way they were all bandaged up and every kid at the pool then wanted to know what happened. Oh, how I yearned to be like everyone else, put on a bathing suit and just jump in the pool! Instead it took a half hour of readying myself to be humiliated before I could go in the water.

And the cherry on top was my nystagmus, which made my eyes shift back and forth in a very pronounced way. So when I wasn't being teased for wearing a bathing cap, kids were asking me what was wrong with my shifty eyes.

I used to hate it when kids would come up to me and say, "Hey, do you know your eyes go back and forth?" Then they'd show me how with a hand motion. I learned to answer back, "No, I didn't. Holy shit, do you think I need a doctor? Hey, stop moving back and forth. Stand still. Did you know you are constantly moving? Aren't you getting tired? Are you nervous about something?"

A lot of kids would totally do a double take and walk away. One kid at overnight camp ran away and threw up by a tree when I used this line on him. A counselor wanted me to clean it up since I was the one who made him upset. At eleven-years-old I had the forethought to say I saw the counselor drunk the night before and if he made me clean up the barf I'd tell the camp director.

I don't really think I knew how ingenious that was. I didn't even know what being drunk was. But unbelievably the counselor had been drunk and could lose his job for it. So he cleaned the barf and we became big-brother-little-brother due to our secret. And apparently he told the other counselors that I was cool because I started getting a lot of slaps on the back from them along with exclamations that I was "the man."

Overnight camp was the worst, though, because the entire thing was built around sports. It was two months full of activities designed to bore and humiliate me. The entire camp got to see me at my worst: bathing cap, lack of coordination, fear of being hit by balls and poor eyesight. Everything I hated, plus I got to live with the kids who spent the day telling me how bad I played out on the ball fields, basketball and hockey courts. However, I was always able to find a kid worse off than I was and make fun of him. I could get my whole bunk to join in because I was relentless. I never knew when to stop.

There was this one slightly overweight but hulking big Jewish kid, who was actually a nice guy, named Wayne. However, I got everyone to call him Dwayne and ask him questions about what it was like to be black. At night when the bunk lights went out, I'd be whispering, "Hey Dwayne, when your mom picks you up at the end of camp, do you think it will be in a stolen car?" Then you'd hear a voice from across the bunk in the dark call out, "Hey Dwayne, what do you like better, ribs or fried chicken?" Everybody would be hysterical. Everybody except Wayne.

We were so relentless one day that Wayne went deep into the woods and I heard he contemplated suicide. We were ordered by staff to immediately cease and desist. Of course I couldn't let it go and we all whispered things to him at night in our bunk beds about eating collard greens and driving a pimpmobile when he got older to pick up hoes. We had no idea what "hoes" were. We just watched *Saturday Night Live.*

How could I take so much abuse, know how horrible it feels, and then give it right back to someone else? I knew it was wrong but I couldn't stop myself. I think it was because the one thing I had going for me was a wicked sense of humor. And it was the only thing I had to make people like me, so I thought. I figured if I could take it, Wayne could take it.

But I was getting worried he was going to leave camp because of me. It was too late in the season to find another butt for my jokes.

All the guys loved my Dwayne jokes. I'd make up a new name for him or say something funny and I'd hear people repeating things I said and laughing all day on the basketball courts or inside the dining hall.

But worse than guys not liking me because of my utter ineptness in sports, was that girls hated me, too. I think the guys always mocking me about the bathing cap fueled it, or that the girls saw me trying to play sports and thought it was a riot. One girl actually came up and kicked me in the shins as she made fun of my eyes. Since they were girls, I never fought back. I was always very respectful around them. My maternal grandmother taught me proper etiquette with the opposite sex.

And then one day as a popular girl was haranguing me on a bus ride back from a canoe trip, I figured it out. I turned around in my seat and said, "You just don't like me because I'm Jewish. You hate Jews."

The girl spent the entire half hour ride back to camp proving to me how much she loved Jews and that her best friend was Jewish. Moreover, she decided I was going to be one of her friends, as well, just to prove her open-mindedness.

I couldn't believe it worked. I was sure it would backfire. But in a day before political correctness was in vogue, this little skinny shiksa girl was falling all over herself to be nice to prove she wasn't prejudiced. I think I spurred her on to become a social worker when she got older, just to make sure everyone knew she was a lover of all races. And when she comes home at night she tells her husband how much she hates the "niggers" and "spics" and that "they should learn to help themselves." But, there is this strange white guy named Dwayne who comes into the clinic talking Ebonics and thinks he is black. She only likes him because he's Jewish. She loves Jews.

Am I sorry for how I treated Wayne? Profusely. And he wasn't the only one I taunted growing up. I hate myself for it. Mainly because, of all people, I knew how it felt. I was just so tired of being made fun of that I wanted to shift the focus. The problem was, it was often to another human being. I cringe inside when I think about what an asshole I was. Now I have to live with it. I can never take it back.

I have tried to teach my daughter to be a better person than I and to be kind to everyone. But after getting a look at some of the miscreants in her grade school classes, I've found myself recommending kids to ridicule and giving her the ammunition. The amazing thing about Madeline is that even when she was eight-years-old, she knew it was wrong and wouldn't do it. She thought it was funny, but kept the jokes between the two of us. Sometimes I think she is the adult, not me.

Now that I've established just how bad I was at sports, there was one sport I could actually do reasonably well and enjoyed. My dad had started running in the mid-seventies. He'd do six miles around the neighborhood. I would meet up with him for his last two miles and finish out his run with him. He was hard to keep up with but we both liked it. And I think it was the first time we had a mutual interest in a sport and did it together.

Soon I started running on my own. When I got a little older we were able to do entire runs together, although I could not always keep up with him for the whole distance. But we loved it. We entered local races and I felt for the first time that he was really proud of me. At twelve-years-old I was making a good effort and I enjoyed doing it with him.

It was the best when we started and finished a run together. Then we'd cool down and go over the whole thing, rating its difficulty. And the older we got, the faster I got and the slower he became. I would often pull away from him halfway through the run. I felt bad, but I think he was kind of proud.

Then my dad started having back and knee problems and had to trade running for low impact sports. Suddenly running became bad and "nothing but a way to dish out a horrible punishment to your body." He would constantly scorn me for running more than five miles, which to him was the bewitching point at which my legs and arms would fall off.

But running to me was more than a workout. It lifted my depression and kept me away from smoking cigarettes for twenty years. And because of my obsessive-compulsion, I decided I was going to train for the Long Beach Marathon when I was in my early forties. My dad said the usual, "You're lookin' for nothin' but trouble." But I didn't care. He thought everything in life he couldn't or didn't want to do was inherently bad. And if it cost money it was even worse.

I paid no mind. I was focused on my goal. It takes an enormous amount of time to train for a marathon because you have to run at least three times a week and one run has to be a minimum of sixteen miles. However, I felt like it was something I had to conquer. Naturally, I became compulsive about training. I loved running in San Francisco and although I wasn't fast, I had little trouble doing the high mileage. I felt like I had accomplished so many things as a bipolar man, this was the next frontier. I knew my medication slowed me down and dehydrated me, but I was going to beat it again or at least learn how to work around it. I was always challenging myself on just what I could accomplish.

So that October Debra, our daughter and I made the trip down the coast to Long Beach for the big marathon. Physically, I was ready. However, I was terrified of getting sick or hurt before the race. The night before, we went to a big pasta feed and I stayed away from alcohol. Then I gashed my leg on the bed in the hotel room. Fortunately I got it to stop bleeding, but it looked like hell and throbbed.

That night I set four alarms at five o'clock. I was not about to sleep through the race. When they all went off at the same time I almost had to be peeled off the ceiling. So happy I didn't over sleep, I proceeded to cripple myself by taking the wrong medication.

When I realized it, I panicked. It was like a lightning bolt of anxiety shooting through my body. I sat on the bed freaking out and screaming incoherently to Debra about what I had done. I had come so far and I took the wrong medication. How could I be so stupid?

So then I decided my best bet was to take the right pills, hoping I'd be able to handle it and at least not suffer any depression. However, it was a double dose of certain powerful meds. Very shortly after I could tell my body was a little off. And I was so furious. Why did I do this to myself? Did I jinx myself and not know it? Had I not counted how many times I brushed each tooth the night before? Did I not park the car perfectly symmetrical in the parking space the night before? Was this a blessing because something bad was going to happen in the race and I should give it up?

I wanted to kill myself for what I had done and for the fact that I had done it *to myself.* Then I thought, "What better way to kill myself than running a marathon pumped full of psych meds? Fuck it, I'm running." But what a buzzkill.

Next came the coffee fiasco. I had to have coffee before I ran. I didn't know if it was a physical need or another jinx that I had to satisfy, but I didn't want to tempt fate. So, I went to Starbucks only to find them closed due to an equipment failure. Another sign? I raced back to the hotel in a panic and found the kitchen was not yet open. Then I grabbed a waiter and begged for a cup. He took pity on me and gave me a huge foam cup of coffee. Thank god the coffee made me poop. Not dropping a load before a run is the kiss of death. For sure you'll lose time sneaking around in someone's backyard, trying to fire off a few rounds without the homeowner seeing you or else you'll have to unload in a dirty, overflowing Port-a-Potty along the way.

Fortunately the caffeine masked how out of sorts I felt from the medication overdose. I began to get excited to run and my nerves settled down a bit. I peed a million times just to make sure I didn't have to go during the marathon. I kept checking my bladder over and over to make sure there was not a drop of urine in it. Running when you have to pee is the worst when you are obsessive-compulsive. You can't get your mind off it.

Soon it was off to the races. I had no idea if I could do this. There were so many runners in the best running gear money could buy and all I could think was that I had never gone more than sixteen miles. I stretched out in a big park with all the other runners, said goodbye to Debra and Madeline and made my way to the starting line. I was alone now. It was all me. I just stood there packed against all the other runners smelling their various too-close-for-comfort body odors and waited for the gun to go off. It seemed like forever. My anxiety level was rising again and I was beginning to hope race officials would just point the starting gun at me and fire.

But when the gun cracked I purposely took it real slow. I decided for the first half that no matter how many people passed me, I was going to keep a slow pace. I turned on my iPod, which had six hours of my favorite rock and blues mixed together, and lost myself in the music, scenery and excitement. I ran on the beach, the freeway, and through the city of Long Beach. I was enjoying the scenery, the cheering crowds and the people offering fruit and water to the runners. I was so proud to be running this marathon that it made me use my very best running posture, as if anyone cared.

I took water on the fly at every mile and used the nutritional paste I brought with me religiously. It was starting to get hot when we hit the thirteen-mile mark. I could see the half-marathon runners going down the finish line chute, getting applause and cheers for their efforts. I ran off in another direction with the twenty-six-milers where there was a lot less fanfare. I thought to myself, "This is where I'll see what I'm made of." I picked up my pace ever so slightly.

Running a marathon is like assisted suicide. The City of Long Beach race organizers do everything they can to help you reach the finish line. If you drop dead before you finish, it's your problem. You sign a release. They just want to put on a good race.

There was four-mile stint around mile sixteen where I was running on unshaded blacktop with the Southern California sun beating down on me and draining all my energy. I was loping along at a snail's pace. I watched people sit down on the side of the road not looking so good. I also saw a few bone wagons carting people away. I started hearing my dad's voice saying, "You see? I told you the body was not meant for this. Now you are learning the hard way. Just give it up."

I slowed down to a quick-paced walk and popped out my iPod earbuds. My music had become annoying after three hours. And then I decided it: "I am not giving up even if they have to take me away on a stretcher." I had no idea how prophetic my words would be.

Again, I began running and never stopped. At mile twenty I knew I was going to finish. I kept telling myself six miles was nothing. "Ain't nothin' but a thang," as the black sergeant said to an enlisted man in the movie *Hamburger Hill*, who had the lower portion of his body blown off by a bouncing betty in the jungles of Vietnam. I was having some really random thoughts.

Running along the ocean promenade on mile twenty-four was where I fucked myself. I was basically delirious from the heat and extreme exhaustion. I thought I was on mile twenty-five and poured on my finishing kick. Halfway through it I learned I still had a mile to go after that. But I was spent. I had nothing left. I could feel my body shutting down. "I'm still finishing," I told myself. "I'm not quitting."

As I ran down the crowd-infested chute toward the finish line, I felt like it kept getting farther away. "What the fuck?" I kept thinking, "When I get to that finish line I'm going to kick its ass in front of everyone for screwing with my head. I'm gonna fuck-up that yellow bastard! Then let's see who's laughing!" I was mad at everything. I wanted to kick the asses of the cops who were directing traffic.

With ten yards to the finish line my body quit on me. My legs became Jell-O. I couldn't even muster the strength to pump my arms. Dizzy and disoriented, I went down. I tried to get up but I couldn't. I had not an ounce of energy in my body. And I was a few yards short of the finish line. I looked like Gumby on a bad day.

The next thing I knew some guys and girls in orange vests gripped me under my arms and were standing me up to see if I could walk it in. I went down immediately when they let go. My vision was starting to fade. I was very disoriented. Then a male voice said, "You wanna finish the race, don't you?"

"Yes! I want to finish. Please." I was so close.

So the orange crew picked me up under each arm and dragged me over the finish line. I heard cheering and felt a medal being placed around my neck. The next thing I knew I was in a wheelchair headed for the hospital tent with all the medical staff asking me a million questions at once.

My temperature was 105, my pulse was irregular and I was badly dehydrated. I was a candidate for the hospital. But instead they stuck me with two IV's, dumped a trashcan of ice all over me and called Debra's cell phone. I was in utter glory for finishing the race so none of this bothered me.

I must have looked horrible when Debra and Madeline arrived, except for the big smile on my face. I showed them the medal and told them I finished. They missed the spectacle of me being dragged over the finish line. Debra couldn't believe I finished and was genuinely happy for me. I also got the feeling she'd had enough of me being scraped up off the ground and being taken to the hospital, even if this wasn't a mental crisis.

After four hours in the tent and a few friends coming in to have their picture taken with me lying in ice with all the IV's, they let me go back to my hotel. By evening Debra, Madeline and I went out to dinner and I was drinking beer like nothing had happened. Except that my legs were so stiff I could barely bend them. But all in all, I felt pretty good.

When I heard that my time for the race was four hours and forty-five minutes, I was thrilled. I knew I could do better the next time if I trained a little bit differently and didn't take an overdose of medication before the race. When I announced in the car ride back to San Francisco that I wanted to do the L.A. Marathon, there was silence.

The Plumpsters

When we were in our thirties, Debra and I joined a Jewish social group through our synagogue. The group is called a Havurah and it is designed to match couples all around the same age and place in life. The idea is to share your lives with one another, becoming Jewish pizzanos forever. All my life I wanted to be a Jewish Guido with a posse of Jews I could trade insults with, sitting on the hoods of our Honda Accords in front of a local deli raving about the corned beef and wearing our wife beaters.

I had always denounced religions of all kinds and been a strong proponent for my atheist views, but I liked the Jewish culture and wanted to experience some of that kinship like the Italians have. So we were set up with five other couples, none of us married or with children.

We would all get together and play poker, go out to dinner, celebrate Jewish holidays, help each other with home renovation projects, so on and so forth.

Eventually some couples moved away and we became friendlier with others, finally ending up close with only two Havurah families. By the mid- nineties, we all had kids and were homeowners.

One couple had two little girls. The husband was the guy who studied vaginas in strip clubs and was completely henpecked. The wife was never too shy to tell you that the meat was too dry and she hated your selection of dinner music when invited over for a meal.

The other couple I called the Plumpsters. To this day, I truly like the husband. No matter how you look at it, he didn't have a mean bone in his body, in spite of the fact that he dropped me like an HIV-infested needle when Debra and I split. But we always had a lot to talk about and took an annual trip to Reno where we went to strip bars, stayed out until the wee hours and got so loaded we couldn't find our hotel.

Then there was his wife: overweight, no neck, mom jeans, short dish-like hairstyle and as controlling as the big boss man on a chain gang. I wanted to take her hair off her head and play a round of ultimate Frisbee with it. When I talked to her I felt like a little kid speaking to one of my parents' friends. She frowned on everything I did, as I was not a good family man in her eyes. The lady made me nervous. I was always waiting for her to tell my mom I was being naughty. I only tolerated her because I thought her husband was a quality person.

The couple spawned two little bowling balls, one boy exactly Madeline's age and one boy a few years behind. When the boys weren't crying, whining and fighting with each other, they were eating. As a matter of fact, they were always eating. And they were not exactly organic, free-range kids. Even in their mini-van mom would make sure they had an ample supply of chips, high fructose drinks and chocolaty snacks. God forbid they drove around the block without each of them downing a bag of Fritos and a Sprite.

Since mom had a butterball figure, she made sure her husband had a gut, too, so she wouldn't be lonely eating ice cream out of the carton for breakfast while the back of her pants flapped in the wind as she passed gas. I began privately calling them the Plumpsters. Even Debra called them that a few times, so I knew they fit the bill.

About a year before Debra and I separated I started pulling away from our friends. As I mentioned earlier, their lives seemed boring to me and I just didn't care about anything they had to say. I didn't care about new additions to their homes, the used SUV that took five months of ruminating over to purchase, the trials and tribulations of climbing their corporate ladders, etc. My mood stabilizers and emotional state left me completely uninterested in anything civilized. All I wanted was just to drink. Bottles of beer danced in my head.

And, I couldn't stand to hear Debra talk about her job, annoying family, plans for Madeline or anything that would cause her to emit that laugh of hers. I didn't know if I was getting weirder or things were getting more unbearable.

Between talking about work, the Plumpster boys wailing for want of a hydrogenated-fat-and-preservative infusion, my daughter telling me she was bored and me commiserating with her, the only thing that got me through one of those evenings was getting ripped. And these were they type of people who, when you visited, always had five kinds of ice cream and cake in the house but only half a six-pack of beer. Where were their priorities?

But nothing was worse than our Christmas time family trips with the Plumpsters to Lake Tahoe where we rented a house together for a week to go skiing. Especially that last year, when I realized my whole life was about to change and wondered if I had the mental wherewithal to make it through. Something told me this was going to be an especially strange trip.

Getting there was always tense. The cars were always packed with food but Mother Plumpster still needed things from the supermarket when we got to Tahoe. Then we'd all look around the rental house and almost always yield the better bedroom to the Plumpsters. Even when Debra made all the plans, we always somehow felt beholden to the Plumpsters. The kids would all stay in a room together where the oldest (seven-years-old at the time) of the Plumpster boys would show my seven-year-old daughter his penis. Between the whining and the food obsessions, his future definitely includes some time on a psychiatrist's couch.

The rest of the week consisted of the kids being in ski school, Debra and I walking around the resort killing time, Pappy Plumpster skiing with a friend and Mamma Plumpster visiting the parents of a friend. For some reason I found her hanging out with parents very annoying. Who spends that much time with the *parents* of a friend? Unless you relate more to the parents. She did look and act their age.

At night Mamma and Debra would cook, Pappy Plumpster and I would clean up and then we'd all watch a science fiction movie I had no interest in while dessert was served. I'd usually get drunk and fall asleep until it was over and cross-off another day on the mountain of pain.

Somehow I knew this would be the last trip to Tahoe as a family. I told Debra I would not do this again with the Plumpsters. She said she knew. And for some reason the next night we were the closest with one another we had been in over a year. It was very strange, though, because I felt like I was saying goodbye to her, not like I was making love to her. I loved her but I knew I was going away.

The next day we were killing time walking around the resort and we stopped in a jewelry store. Debra saw a beautiful jade ring. I suddenly wanted her to have it and got it for her. She teared up when I put it on her finger. It would be the last thing I ever gave her. Kind of a going away gift. None of this was spoken, though.

Later that day I went to the gym. I was scared of how I was going to afford a divorce and felt that old familiar depression start to drop on me like a cold, wet blanket. However, word of divorce was never even spoken.

I knew exercise was a good antidepressant so I went inside the gym and worked out until every part of my body ached. I was still depressed, but I felt more in control of my emotions and a little better about myself. "If it's divorce, it's divorce. Millions of guys in much worse financial shape than me get through this. I can handle it if they can," I thought. But I was also worried about my mental state. Could my head handle it? This was a big trigger, conjuring up all sorts of emotions.

Debra asked for the divorce when we got home on New Year's Day 2008. She was positive I was having an affair with my dentist, was drinking too much and basically had a death wish every time I got behind the wheel of my Mustang. She felt alone and detached from me. She was doing what I didn't have the backbone to do by letting me go. I was ruining her life by not pulling the trigger and she, once again, had to be the adult.

I never saw the Plumpsters again.

Blue Years Eve

Blue Year's Eve can be the worst night of the year. You can't stop it from happening. However, you can control how you handle it. Whether you're a guy in your teens in New York City or in your forties in Idaho, all you can think of is meeting hot girls, getting them drunk and having sex with them when they pass out, regardless of the fact that they have vomit all over them.

What usually ends up happening is that you spend half the night looking for the ever-elusive ultimate party and finally find it. Unfortunately, it turns out to be a hot, sweaty, sausage-fest of freshly crew-cutted young men in Christmas sweaters sucking down light beer, crowding around two or three semi-hot girls like low hanging fruit. So you end up at some bar commiserating with all the other slobs who struck out, spend way too much money, get terribly drunk and accidentally offend someone, causing you to make a hasty exit and drive home with your lights off. You're completely wrecked and barely avoid mowing down a traffic cop and getting arrested. Then you wake up in the morning feeling sick, hating yourself for spending all that money and trying to recall who you embarrassed yourself in front of and just how badly. And that is why they call it Blue Year's Eve.

If you're bipolar it's even worse. You have to take medication that makes you even more hung over and sleepy the next day. Your depression is ten times worse and everything that happened the night before makes you suicidal. You feel like you have no friends, no money and no self-respect. What is supposed to be the greatest night of the year leads to a day clouded by depression and angst. And what's worse, the same thing happened the year before and, like a fool, you did it again. Moreover, you will probably do it again next year.

Blue Year's Eve was like a slot machine to me. Every year I'd put my money and hair gel into it and every year I'd bust out. But my obsessive-compulsive disorder kept telling me, "Keep playing. This is the year I am going to win big."

Here are some things I have done on Blue Year's Eve before I realized I was probably never going to hit the jackpot.

In high school I was reuniting with my girlfriend with whom I was having a long distance relationship while she was attending college in Texas. The funny part was we had only met each other twice that summer and were instantly spending countless hours on the phone for the next six months, planning our Blue Year's Eve love affair. I was experiencing flat out OCD symptoms and couldn't stop myself. I was obsessed about having the escape of a girlfriend from a life with an angry, overly cynical father and school I couldn't stand in Bethlehem, Pennsylvania.

So we ushered in the Blue Year in a flophouse in a bad neighborhood in Philadelphia, leaving us both relatively broke. We drank, smoked some pot and then the big anticipated sexual union turned out to be her telling me how once she was almost raped and could no longer have orgasms. She was also dry as a burned-out creek bed, her vagina smelled like cigarettes, and in a dark room it was still hard kidding myself – she didn't have much sex appeal. The gunfire down on the street below didn't help, either. When all was said and done, Blue Year's Day I was hung-over, out of money and I still had to entertain a slightly overweight, haggard-looking nineteen-year-old who kept tearing up with one of those, "I was almost raped stories." It seems like every girl has one. It's a badge of honor.

Then there was the Blue Year's in college where I found myself sitting in a hotel room with a drunken girl whose hand was over her mouth as she spewed green vomit out between her fingers. It was like a sprinkler system, the way it sprayed. I was fascinated. But when the guy she was kissing would not start making out with her again, she went berserk and started screaming, crying and tearing up the room. So my girlfriend and I put her in her car and pointed her toward home, but we were somewhat responsible and followed her at a distance to make sure she made it ok. Or, just in case we had to anonymously notify her parents that she'd been arrested for drunk driving.

Then back at the hotel, between cleaning up and all the money we had to pay in damages, I was tired, broke, hung-over and had had absolutely no fun. I didn't even really like the girl I was dating. She really liked me and because I suddenly thought I might never again in my life find another girl who liked me, I tried to be thankful for what I had. "I mean, shouldn't we all be grateful for what we are given?" I thought to myself. She did have a vagina and breasts.

Another Blue Year's Eve in Philadelphia when I was still in high school, my best friend and I were drunk and going to visit a girl I really liked at where she was babysitting for the night. I was actually crazy about her and I know she liked me, too. The minute we got there my friend, Joe, was trying to put his arm around her, kiss her and grab her ass nonstop. Finally she said we had to go. As we got to the back door Joe pushed me out and then suddenly shut it, locking himself and the girl inside. From behind the glass he mouthed, "Wait for me," and then pulled down the curtain.

I was furious. I knew she didn't really like him but in my drunken state was sure he was going to score. Joe was always abusive to me yet we were best friends. After all, I thought, best friends were hard to come by. "Shouldn't we all be grateful for what we were are given?" So what if Joe did have a penchant for tackling me to the ground and punching me in the back of the head completely unprovoked? Or, made me treat him to everything and never paid me back? I was downright lucky to have a pal like Joe, I told myself. I actually used to call him Juice because one day he tried to fart in my face while I was sleeping and he accidentally sprayed diarrhea on me. But I couldn't call him Juice in public or I'd be on the ground in seconds.

Joe also had a fantastic collection of *Playboy* magazines passed down to him by his dad. It was a privilege to lay on our stomachs side by side on one of his twin beds and each jerk off to one. The only rule was that you could not look at the other person or make any noise. If I accidentally commented on a girl or simply sneezed, Joe would grab a baseball bat and attempt to beat me into unconsciousness, so he could finish jerking off under the illusion that he was alone. Now that was a buzzkill. But I was grateful for the privilege of being allowed to mastur-bate with one of Joe's *Playboys.*

Anyway, I had passed out on the sidewalk for I don't know how long until Joe came out and dragged me to my feet, telling me it was after midnight. Then I had to listen to his diatribe about his conquest the entire walk back to his apartment. I doubted it was true because this girl was not a slut, but hearing it cut me like a knife anyway. And since he was broke, I had bankrolled the whole night. In essence, I took Joe out for the evening, fed him pizza, paid for his video games, beer, weed, cigars and then let him play "slap and tickle" with the girl *I* liked. You can imagine how good I felt the next day.

More Blue Year's Eve fun: I was working for the classical music station in Philadelphia. I was extremely depressed. I had stopped taking Elavil because of the sexual side effect of basically not being able to feel an orgasm and the new medication was not doing the trick psychologically. But for some reason I was still taking it and I was functionally suicidal. I was living with Jacqui but we had broken up so we were in separate rooms. To make matters worse, her separate room often had a guest in it. That I could barely tolerate. Especially if I'd run into the guy wiping off his dick on one of my towels in the bathroom.

So I decided instead of getting drunk and going broke I'd work on a catering crew with a friend of mine at a huge, high-end Blue Year's Eve party, in a big, stately old hall called the Philadelphia College of Physicians. I worked like a dog from noon to 4:00 A.M. First there was the set-up of everything being brought in by trucks. Then there was the preparation. There was serving at the cocktail party, where I carried around the garbage tray so rich people could discard their martini napkins, toothpicks and unfinished hors d'oeuvre. One idiot guest actually took one off the trash tray and put it in his mouth. I didn't bother telling him it was garbage. And one guest recognized me from my professional career in radio, which was nothing short of humiliating.

Then there was serving the dinner and dessert. After the last ass-holes went home, we washed dishes and silverware and put everything back into the trucks.

I hated every single miserable moment of it: people yelling instruc-tions at me, rude guests, lifting and cleaning. I was tired and so depressed I felt like crying half the time. And when I got home at 4:30 A.M. there was Jacqui sitting alone at the kitchen table, smoking a cigarette and tell-ing me about how much money she'd spent and what a miserable night she had.

And for a moment my cloud of depression lifted slightly. I, too, had had an awful night. However, I had started out with no expectations of a good one so I was not disappointed. Plus, I had money in my pocket and I was not going to be hung-over in the morning. Then it dawned on me that this was how you do Blue Year's. If you don't go out and try to have the Blue Year's of all Blue Year's Eves, you won't spend too much money, risk embarrassing yourself and wake up depressed. And from 1990 on that is how I have done Blue Year's Eve. No expectations, no disappointments.

Next was my first Blue Year's in San Francisco. I volunteered to go to an orientation to work on the Suicide Hotline. I have no idea why, because sometimes I felt like I was the one who needed to be calling it, but I guess I felt if I could help others with their depression it would be a cathartic experience for me. However, I never followed up on it. I felt like me on the other end of the phone with someone suicidal would be a sham. I can hear it now: "Look, your life does suck. And I think every-body has a right to kill his or herself. Maybe this is your time." Audible bang.

I met a girl at the meeting and she asked what I was doing that evening to ring in the Blue Year, and invited me to join her group of friends at a get-together. I declined and said I would be busy fixing my road bike that was in a million pieces in my studio apartment. This was a lie, but it sounded so nonchalant I went with it. I wanted to stay in and adhere to my new plan for Blue Year's Eve.

Apparently it also made me sound independent and bold because we ended up going out a few times after that. Until, of course, she turned out to be a nymphomaniac who smelled like Vicks VapoRub, had virtually no breasts and bought her plain white panties at the checkout stand in Walmart. And the only way to get rid of her was to do something to make her hate me. So, I invited her out to dinner with my equally weird friend Bob, the vitamin salesman. When she figured out it was a set-up she stormed out of the restaurant and left me an angry barrage of phone messages. Poor Bob just sat there in his Gilligan's Island fishing hat and big rectangular, brown plastic "dad glasses" clutching his brief case of vitamins with a bewildered look on his face.

On Blue Year's 2009 I lost my way and strayed from my teachings. I was newly single and dating this girl I met online. We had gone out a few times and all she did was tell me how our relationship was doomed to fail, as were all relationships. She never let me get close to her and was always prophesizing at what point we would be over.

When I had about all I could take, I stopped seeing her. Then out of nowhere she called to apologize and wanted to spend Blue Year's Eve with me. She promised not be a psychiatric case. So against my better judgment I made reservations at an expensive restaurant and bought great wine so we could go back to my apartment and watch the fireworks from my Nob Hill balcony, a fancy neighborhood in San Francisco that I was living in by the skin of my teeth.

The $300 dinner was so-so. My date was a bit subdued, but well behaved enough for me to think this could work. When we got back to my apartment I made her comfortable on the couch, put on some good music, lit a few candles, opened a nice bottle of wine and pulled back the curtains so we could see the fireworks show.

Then she fell apart. Hysterical crying about some Mexican busboy she couldn't help being in love with and obsessing about. It took me a minute to believe she was serious. The carrying on was almost comical. I had not one ounce of empathy toward her.

A consummate gentleman, I helped her off the couch and on with her coat. Then I walked her to the front door and wished her the best of luck finding a cab home on Blue Year's Eve and said I sincerely hoped she had some cash. Then I eased her out into the hallway and shut my door. I could hear her crying all the way to the elevator. She sounded a little like Lucille Ball. "Whah, Ricky!"

To make sure I had completely eliminated this mistake from my apartment building's premises, I called down to the doorman and said a crying girl was about to appear in the lobby. "Manny, she's a freak," I said. "Don't let her back up. Do me a favor and dump her in a cab."

Manny started laughing. "Mr. Goodman, you're too funny. She looked nice when you brought her up. I saw you kiss her in the elevator." I hated those elevator cameras. The doormen were always getting their thrills from them.

"Blue Year's Eve, Manny. She was wearing a mask." I hung up.

I was drunk, depressed and out over $300. I also felt like a fool for letting her back into my life. What happened to my Blue Year's rule that had served me so well?

So now I'm back on the Blue Year's wagon. I don't think it's advisable with my bipolar condition to get all worked up about an evening that carries such a heavy warning sign on it. My wife asked for a divorce on Blue Year's Day 2008; shouldn't that have given me a clue about this evil time of year? Sure, I wanted it, too. But having it happen on Blue Year's means you'll never forget the exact day your marriage ended. It's like my daughter's second day of pre-school being on 9-11-2001. Nobody ever remembers his or her kid's *second* day of pre-school by date, unless it was an important date. Then it smacks you in the head every year whether you like it or not.

After my experience with the crazy girl, I decided to ask my doctor if I could be put in a coma every year, December 31st through January 2nd. This way I'd miss the whole fucking depressing ordeal. But it was not to be. I would have to learn to manage it on my own.

And so after a life of frantic quests for the perfect Blue Year's Eve met with disappointment and despair, I stay home on Blue Year's where I can't get into any trouble or spend too much money. A self-imposed curfew for my own good. With bipolar you have to learn your triggers and steer clear of them. No matter how much medication you're on, you have to do a little of the work yourself. And part of my work is staying out of situations I know I'll regret. It's taken me a lifetime to figure this one out. Maybe this tale can save you some time.

Happy Blue Year!

Thank You for Your Support

Ipopped the clutch and rumbled into the parking garage in my brand new convertible Mustang GT California Special, complete with hood scoop, side vents and dual chrome exhaust pipes. I took my place in the second row among the Priuses, Hondas, late model BMW three series, Volvos and Subarus. I wasn't feeling the love anymore.

Thanks to the chatty parking attendant, the entire radio and TV station knew in no time that I had broken the unspoken covenant and had bought a muscle car. I guess if you work in the garage when someone gets a new car it can really make your day.

I'm also sure in some people's minds they were questioning whether someone like me should be allowed to represent public television and radio with a car like that. I obviously didn't care about the environment or the plain-Jane politically correct values its employees were expected to uphold.

After all, I had just gotten in trouble from some woman a few cubicles over for calling the $10 salad I got from the restaurant across the street the "bend over salad," as it wasn't worth the price. Although my manager saw the humor in it, I was still forbidden to utter the blatantly offensive words again. Thank you for your support.

Now here I was with a car that could bring the "man-slack-wearing" public broadcasting ladies to tears. And all the men in their own dress slacks, in competition to see who could wear the smallest spectacles,

171

wondered why I didn't get a Beamer. I automatically dislike anyone who calls a BMW a Beamer.

I had taken this job soliciting underwriting, which is what public broadcasting calls advertising, for the predominate public radio and television stations in San Francisco, and the nation for that matter. I thought it would be a more supportive environment than the commercial broadcasting cesspool of sleaze I had been swimming around in for the past sixteen years. It seemed a kinder and gentler place where people were more concerned about the quality and integrity of the programming. Instead of thanking clients for their business, we thanked them for their support. I loved this twist on the sales process. Sure, the pay was not as good, but the less-pressured atmosphere and the idea of working for a good cause seemed well worth it.

As I've said before, any kind of sales is the worst possible profession someone with bipolar illness can embark upon. It comes complete with indiscriminate rejection, fierce competition (internally and externally), impossible deadlines and unpredictable income. There should be a pill for it. And public broadcasting appeared to be that compound.

But the station was slowly trying my patience with their political correctness and self-congratulatory nature. Twice I was called out on the carpet for wearing too much cologne. My manager had to speak with me about that, because my accusers preferred to remain anonymous. People do not confront one another in public broadcasting. They tattle like little girls, and then have their managers or human resources do it. Thank you for your support.

This was actually an amusing request. Would they rather me not shower and pepper the office with foul body odor every time I decided to get up and walk around? I decided to ignore the request and dowsed myself with even more Dolce & Gabbana in the morning. I mean, it wasn't like it was Aqua Velva. And, I figured, what was going to happen to me? I'd get fired for good hygiene and a pleasant smell?

This relaxed atmosphere I had chosen as a better option for my bipolar was now starting to frustrate me to no end with its self-righteous attitude and standard response of "it can't be done." The phrase was thrown around like a discus. A client asked for an unusual but reasonable request in the real world from our bookkeeping department. "It can't be done." I need an easy edit done on a Monday for a TV commercial? "It's not Wednesday so it can't be done." My client generously gave us four new cars immediately delivered to the station on trade but needs a check for the taxes, pronto. "It can't be done." Thank you for your support.

And when I'd ask why it couldn't be done I'd get the same response: "We're [name of station]. We have never done it that way. It can't be done. The client will have to wait." That's when my head would shoot off my body leaving a vapor trail like a Blue Angels jet plane, flying around the station making mean faces at everyone.

People started to get annoyed with me because I knew most things could be done and I'd make them do it. In some cases I'd just forge documents myself. In other cases I'd go to management and tell them how much money we were losing because of the office's "it can't be done" attitude. This was no way to run a business.

Then I started getting passed over for things. I got no recognition at the all-staff meeting when they handed out awards for people who had given five years of service, as I had at the time. Then my manager took the credit for trading with a solar company to put panels on our roof and getting a $50,000 rebate check from Pacific Gas and Electric, when I was the one who did the deal. Finally, I was the last to get my own office and it was furnished with an old-broken-down desk from the bowels of the basement, making it look like the squad room from *Barney Miller*, a 1970s sitcom. Everyone else had new furniture. I had to ask the facilities manager myself if I could have everything everyone else had furnishings-wise. My bosses didn't seem to care. Thank you for your support.

I had several incidents over my course of employment there when I attempted suicide and either ended up in the hospital or at home on medical leave for several weeks while I got my head back together. And although it was supposed to be kept a secret, when I returned to work everybody in my department seemed to know I had had some sort of psychological breakdown. Coming back to the office and having everyone welcome me with those inquisitive looks on their faces was unbearable. While their mouths were saying, "I'm glad you're feeling better," their eyes were asking, "So, did you really try to kill yourself? Did they pump your stomach? Did you have to wear a strait jacket? Were you locked in a padded room?" Thank you for your support.

But I stayed at this job for the longest of any other in my life. The bottom line was, it was still better than the degenerate world of commercial media sales. And I was working for public broadcasting, a cause I believe in. Plus, until I could find something else, quitting in a bad economy was a really stupid idea. So I had to learn to cope. Again there was no pill for this. I had to do it on my own.

Sure, I could go to my psychiatrist and demand an adjustment in my medication in an effort to numb myself to my frustrations. And I'm pretty sure I could convince him to do it. But at this stage in my life I knew I'd only be kidding myself; I felt okay and all I'd be chasing was a buzz that I probably wouldn't find. In fact, I'd probably screw up the balance of the medication I had achieved. This would cause me to regress and before you'd know it I'd be sitting in my bipolar group meetings getting tips on how to get government assistance so my fat ass didn't have to work anymore, and I could fill my days going to all kinds of "complaint" groups.

So I decided to work with my psychologist to learn to control my own thinking. And to be honest, I thought this was complete bullshit when she suggested it. I was the most OCD person in the world. If I wanted a new car, I would ruminate over it, crafting an argument why I had to have it *immediately*, no matter how bad an idea it was. The urge was uncontrollable and completely dominated my thoughts. Then I'd buy the car and immediately started hating myself for making such a terrible financial decision. And I was going to learn to control my thoughts?

Funny thing is that I did learn, to a certain degree. I couldn't make things that dominated my mind go away completely, but I could get them out of my head for a period of time. And when they swooped back in for another attack, they weren't quite as potent.

Take a manager I had at the station. He was a little man of Japanese heritage with no people skills whatsoever. He was a salesperson like me and got the managerial job by default because nobody else wanted it. But he was constantly haunted by the fact that his title was "Team Leader" and not "Vice President of Sales and Marketing" like his predecessor, due to a legal issue. It was fun to watch him fuming in his office behind the glass in his ill-fitting Brooks Brothers suit and mismatched shirt and tie, with cufflinks that looked like they had the Target logo on them. Not to mention the little 2.0 spectacles he wore which magnified his eyes, making him look like a scary bug from an old Japanese monster movie.

He also loved to compare clothing. His suit was always more expensive than mine. I bought my shirts in department stores and his were custom made. The colors I wore were too brash and his were more classic. The fact of the matter was that when I die, if they try to bury me in a suit similar to one he would wear, I'll come back to life, climb out of the coffin, smack the undertaker in the head and run over to the Men's Wearhouse for a suit that doesn't make me look like a country club reject for all eternity.

My manager also locked his door every time he left his office, even for a second, like it was filled with gold and silver. And he spent his days emailing me and walking into my office literally yelling about things I was not doing right on our new computer inventory and collections system. He constantly wanted me at his beck and call to blame things on, so much so that I couldn't even talk to a client on the phone or go out on the road and make a sales call, which was the exact opposite of what he should have wanted. Thank you for your support.

It got to the point where I had to change my thinking, because I'd sit there stewing in my office during the day and then go home to get drunk and stoned at night. So I decided, what was the worst possible thing that could happen to me if I just did my job the right way and ignored his over-the-top harassment? Getting fired. And since I was going to rip the lapels off his Brooks Brother's suit and shove them up his ass if I didn't relax, I figured this wasn't a bad option.

Consequently, I'd come into my office, doused in cologne, shut my door and do my work. Sometimes my manager would stand outside my interior window trying to get my attention and I'd just wave him away. I also stopped responding to any email from him I deemed ridiculous. And when he gave me false deadlines, I just ignored them.

The more I did this the nuttier it made him. Whenever we'd finally connect he didn't know what to scold me about first. Then I'd just go out on sales calls or leave at the end of the day and shut that part of my world off. My rationale was the day was done, there was nothing I could do by ruminating about work at home, so I'd enjoy my evening and deal with whatever came my way in the morning.

It became so much fun jerking that little bastard around that I had to stop myself from going overboard. How to make someone *else* lose his or her mind was not the goal of the therapy I had learned. You see, I had been forwarding all of the crazy client phone calls to him so I could hear him lose his temper and scream. Thank you for your support.

I stopped short of disguising my voice and calling him myself, proclaiming I heard he was pronouncing the Japanese word for a type of wine called "Sake" incorrectly. He would freak out if you did not pronounce "Sake" the Japanese way. Did I mention he was born in the United States?

Learning to control my thinking was basically how I learned to deal with working for the station in general. Being one of the premier public broadcasting stations in the country, they suffer from the god complex and an inbred compulsion to cut off their noses to spite their faces. It took me a long time to realize that most things "really can't be done" because management places self-imposed restrictions on themselves, make poorly- thought-out choices and are basically blinded by greed for underwriting dollars, never giving enough consideration to the consequences. Thank you for your support.

All this eventually caused me to resign without another job in a horrible economy. But you have an incompetent sales manager with upper level management who lost touch with their audience and it is not such a special place to work anymore. Thank you for your support.

And the completely out-of-touch, 1980s-style power-tie wearing program director who looks like he has a Brillo Pad hanging from his chin would be sent to the Cannes Film Festival every year, only to come back and slop the same tired British comedies and re-runs of *The American Experience* on the air. More of an embarrassment to all of PBS than just our station, he was actually voted program director of the year by his industry peers. I was dumbstruck when I heard the news.

With a back office comprised of a skinny, annoying, not-as-funny-as-he-thinks sarcastic guy wearing tennis shorts all year round, a balding Iranian man who loves to tell you what you did wrong but not how to fix it, and an engineering staff who won't even let you turn on a DVD player without assistance, it's a wonder the stations manage to stay on the air. You should turn on the television station and just see employees in the studio fighting one another.

As for the radio station, in spite of being top dog in the market my former manager was doing everything in his power to dismantle it. His specialty was thumbing his nose at clients, walking around the office teaching people how to pronounce Japanese words properly and mismanaging on-air inventory until there was nothing left for anyone to sell. He also liked to spend time with females in marathon closed-door office sessions for no particular reason, except for the fact that they were obligated to sit there and listen to the boss.

So this public broadcaster never lived up to what it promised me or its viewers and listeners. Moreover, if this is the premier public broadcaster in the country, I can't imagine what other public stations are like in smaller markets. Are they just like this but with less money?

I am not angry at the station. I believe something good comes out of even bad experiences. There I learned valuable, non-medication-related coping skills I didn't think I had. And the fact that I wasn't sorry to be leaving confirmed I made the right choice. Thank you for your support.

The Jewish Thang

I remember sitting next to my Dad in the synagogue while he hummed along to the Hebrew prayers and songs while I played with the tassels on his prayer shawl, called a tallis. I'd look around the synagogue and see all the "real" Jews following along in the prayer books and uttering all the Hebrew words. My dad hummed his way through Rosh Hashanah and Yom Kippur services, ate a little matzah at Passover time, forced me to go to Hebrew School three times a week and all in all he felt pretty good about his commitment to Judaism.

My mother was worse. Being Jewish was just a stamp of quality to her. It had nothing to do with religion. She usually found a physical excuse to avoid sitting in shule. "The doctor says the seats are not good for my back." Or, "I have this condition where my nose keeps running and I can't sit in services."

When she did go to High Holiday services, which was the only time she could imagine setting foot inside a synagogue, she would talk the whole time. Once the Rabbi stopped mid-prayer and told her to "shut up or get out."

Since my brother lived with her when he turned thirteen, which is Bar Mitzvah age, she just had a Friday night "dessert ceremony" for him in a reformed temple. Reformed Judaism is Judaism light. Most of the services are in English and they are kept short for people who have small attention spans but still want to be seen as pious Jews.

My brother Andrew barely did any time in Hebrew school so he couldn't really strut about the temple holding the Torah belting out prayers, and the laid back reformed Rabbi was more concerned with how well Andy's suit fit than what he knew about Judaism. I spent most of the time in the parking lot smoking pot with my second cousin, Richie.

Unfortunately, I was raised conservative while my parents were still together when it was my time to get Bar Mitzvahed. I had to lead prayers and sing my Haftorah portion with my crackling adolescent voice. It consisted of a Friday night service and a four-hour Saturday service. I now consider it child abuse. And, the Rabbi couldn't have cared less about my suit. Plus, mid-Friday-night-service, the cantor more or less leaned over to me as we were sitting on the pulpit and whispered he was glad I was done with Hebrew school, because if he had to see me three times a week any longer he thought he'd have to kill me.

It's not that I had no respect for my religion; I had and have no respect for any religion. And I realized this at a very young age. I grew up extremely depressed. Not only was I chemically depressed, but I was depressed about the way my parents treated me, living in small town Pennsylvania, not being like all the other kids with my poor eyesight and fragile mentality, being ostracized in regular school and then forced to go to Hebrew school afterward for a second helping of torment.

Being Jewish was just one more burden to bear. And I felt like it was a needless handicap. It didn't make me feel better, it made me feel worse. I was ostracized because of it in regular school and in Hebrew school I was low Jew on the totem pole because my family was less than observant, yet they threw me in with the yamaka-wearing piranhas anyway.

Judaism is the same as all other religions; you waste all your time praying to something that nobody can prove exists and then interpret everyday things to be signs from God. What a royal fucking waste of time. I couldn't believe smart people read and believe the bible, but thought things like meditation were pointless. And I couldn't fathom how sitting in a church or synagogue praying for mankind could be better than going out and delivering meals to the poor, donating clothes to Goodwill or spending a year in the Peace Corps. I figured if there was a god, only one religion out of thousands could be right. And I believe the winning god will judge people on their actions and not on how many times they fell to their knees facing east, wailing prayers of praise to his or her holiness.

But being Jewish is a little different than other religions – it's also a culture. And when I grew up and moved out on my own I realized all of a sudden that I wanted to be around other Jews. I found comfort in it. There aren't that many of us in the world. When you are in a strange city and meet one of the tribe, you instantly bond.

What I also learned was that your level of piousness goes right out the window when you are a cultural Jew. If you have embarrassing grandparents, went to college and you or someone in your family is in the jewelry business, you're as good as related. You can trust this person with your life. To hell with keeping kosher and dessert Bar Mitzvahs.

When I was younger being Jewish was a scarlet letter. It was the last thing I wanted to be identified with. I didn't even want to be around other Jews because even my own people made me feel bad about myself.

But now that I am older I look for people with Jewish names with whom I am associated. I can't wait to make that Jewish connection with them. "Hey, are you Jewish? Me, too! Are you from back east? Me, too!" It's even a status symbol to talk about how bad you fucked up in Hebrew school and how your parents had to drag you down the aisle to the pulpit to get Bar Mitzvahed. The whole Jewish paradigm turns upside down when you get older!

So the thing I thought was holding me back the most is actually the thing that has introduced me to some of my favorite people in the world.

How does this all relate to me being bipolar? I'm not exactly sure. But being Jewish was once a huge source of misery for me and now the cultural aspects are something I cherish. I still have it in for those Hassidic fools prancing around in their dreadlocks, black suits and hats, wasting time praying and missing out on a rack of barbequed pork ribs and the Friday night TV line-up because God says "no." They aren't living life, they are forever preparing for death.

Judaism is no longer that stigma which held me back. However, coming to terms with my ethnic heritage doesn't make me less of a klutz or suffer to a smaller degree from bipolar illness. And sometimes when you peg someone as a Jew and they're not, it can be a little embarrassing.

181

It's like mistaking a Hindu for an African American and greeting them in Ebonics.

But I'm not ashamed of being Jewish. So I just fumble through my life and deal with this bipolar illness the best I can. And when I'm depressed and am having a Lorazepam moment, I just repeat to myself, "I've made it through worse." I have come a really long way from sitting in that synagogue with my Dad, vowing to marry a German girl just to get back at my family for forcing religion on me.

Snap Out of It

This is not intended to be a self-help book. I hate and person-ally invalidate the whole psychological "self-help" genre with its companion CDs and DVDs. However, my validation of anything doesn't mean much. I don't have any DVDs or CDs to sell you and writ-ing a book doesn't make me an expert on anything. But when I watch the media-darling, pseudo-psychologists telling me there is no such thing as mental illness, I feel like I just inhaled modeling glue. That not-so-good kind of sick, high feeling, like when you can actually tell brain cells are being destroyed and you know it's your own stupid fault. But I can't stop watching.

Then when they take their homemade simplistic remedies and mete them out with big rotten wooden ladles over the heads of truly sick peo-ple they have told to "snap out of it," I writhe with anger. And then I watch, almost horrified, as the spoonful of bullshit runs down the face of a thirty-four-year-old housewife in Minnesota who has just been told that she doesn't need medication for her suicidal depression, and instead should just start repeating positive affirmations to feel better. It's really tragic when you realize the guru is dealing with a person with a serious problem like he is tinkering around under the hood of '72 Plymouth Valiant.

I also wonder what the pharmaceutical executives are thinking when they see this "snap out of it" crap airing on primetime television where they are spending massive Madison Avenue sponsorship dollars. Do they think these positive affirmations may threaten drug sales? Will "snap out of it" work? Are they tempted to have a Columbus Day special on Lithium just to shore up sales in the bipolar market?

In my inconsequential opinion, getting hooked on modeling glue is actually preferable to listening to a television shrink make a crack mental diagnosis in minutes and "fix" someone right there in front of an entire television audience. If someone has a serious mental illness and one of these media darlings is doling out remedies from the hip, they can literally kill someone by not letting them get the *real* help they need.

True, all of the cures available to relieve bipolar symptoms have side effects that are sometimes almost as bad as the disease itself. And of course the anti-psychotropic drug advocates are only too eager to point this out and claim they are nothing short of poison. But although this adds fuel to the fire for their arguments, it puts people with bipolar in a real bind. Feel better but suffer the side effects for the rest of your life, or teeter on the edge of suicide but not have your hands shake. The direction you take depends on your priorities and personal tolerance. Or you can just "snap out of it" and everything will be grand.

I have had much treatment for mental illness. Over the years the diagnosis and treatments have changed as the science has evolved. Currently, my official diagnosis is "bipolar II with hypomanic episodes." Doctors almost always add an extra illness onto someone with bipolar. Like "bipolar with borderline personality disorder," or, "bipolar with severe mood disorder." I'm waiting for "bipolar with can't-get-it-up-for-my-girlfriend disorder."

But as words they are pretty much a labeling system for something that comes in so many different varieties you can't really label it. We are like snowflakes, as I don't think I've ever seen two bipolars who are exactly alike. The psychiatric community is a little short on cures, but they are great on giving you what I call "disease estimates." I am part of the bipolar community, and my doctor is guessing I happen to have "a hypomanic cherry on top." But I also just think it's human nature to label and categorize things, and psychiatrists and psychologists, regardless of how much they position themselves as gods in fifty-minute sessions, are human, too.

The one thing all of us bipolars have in common is some sort of related disease of the mind. So the cool-sounding bipolar prefix is actually the glue that binds us with this disease of the mind. Some of us are embarrassed about it. Some of us are forthcoming. Some use it as an excuse. Some use it as a reason to challenge themselves. Some won't shut the fuck up about it. And some are just ready to talk about it for the first time.

When the Dust Settled

It's 2011 and a lot of the dust has settled in my life, at least for the time being. You're never in the clear with bipolar illness. My medication could "poop-out" tomorrow for no reason whatsoever. The point is, you have to be prepared for complications along the way.

There will be no more yelling at defenseless suits in closets, losing Cadillacs at a Phillies night game, disappearing in clouds of cigarette smoke and the Queen of Bethlehem has left her throne. All of my grandparents are dead. And, in spite of their idiosyncrasies, I love and miss them all. They were the splash of color in my life, and the only unconditional love I have ever felt aside from my daughter.

My ex-wife, Debra, became one of my closest friends. We talk now with an understanding of one another like we never did during our marriage. Maybe it's because we stripped away all the things that marriage forces upon a couple, such as having to live together. Debra is the most levelheaded person I know and the best mother to my twelve-year old daughter I could ask for. Although she doesn't always do things my way, her intentions are never anything short of well-meaning. It's strange because in some ways I did marry the right woman, I just didn't want what was right. I wanted what was exciting.

Finally, I did get that excitement out of a partner. My fiancée, Lynn, is my greatest cheerleader and soulmate forever. I'm thankful for every day she is in my life. Lynn gave me the confidence to write this book.

We understand each other without a spoken word and she shares my passion for challenges, while also keeping them from consuming me. A talented jeweler and a patient mother to two little girls, the only thing she is bad at is housekeeping. It's not uncommon to find food that is a week old encrusted on the living room coffee table, mutating into something so grotesque that I have to call the coroner to come get it.

But what she lacks in housekeeping skill she makes up in the animal attraction she sends out to me that I simply can't resist, even if I'm buried under one of her pungent unwashed, month-old laundry piles. Thank god for the Crime Scene Cleaning Service! And in spite of this, I find Lynn so breathtakingly attractive I keep wondering when she is going to dump me for a guy named Dirk at the gym. Did I mention she can cook the undies off Martin Yan?

My father is still happily married to the same woman, going on their tenth year of bliss in Center Valley, Pennsylvania, where they not only now have a Starbucks but a new fancy upscale mall, too. We still talk once a week and get together once a year. Cynical and in his seventies, as long as it doesn't involve money we have a good relationship. I believe it's what's in the heart that counts most, and he has nothing but the best intentions. I've moved past what happened to me as a child. If he knew I was bipolar, things might have been different.

My mother is still alive and kicking in Philadelphia. Constantly searching for the ultimate psychotropic cocktail and having unnecessary operations on her various body parts, she keeps herself in a perpetual state of recovery. Her mind comes and goes from hallucinating depression to being completely coherent and delightful. The problem is, you never know what you are going to get when you call. Her brain is like Forrest Gump's box of chocolates.

I gave up a long time ago wishing that she could be the all-American mother and always there for me with a hot apple pie and a big hug. Sometimes when she is doing well I think maybe she is finally okay, and then a week later you want to use her head as a flowerpot. Thank god she has been married to the earless man for over thirty years. He takes wonderful care of her and silently pines away for her meager trust fund. And to give kudos where they belong, although 3,000 miles away, she does her best to keep in contact with my daughter, sending nice little gifts and cards in spite of the fact that her own financial situation is dismal.

My brother Andy is still as funny as ever. Even in the face of a looming divorce and a horrible real estate market (he's a realtor), he's found other streams of income by teaching realtors how to survive in this economy. He also has a nice new apartment and a great girlfriend. It's been hard on his son and daughter, but he is talking with them about it and being a loving father. He sees them almost every day. And Andy and I speak on the phone all the time. We try to get together at least once a year to make fun of people and buy watches we can't really afford. He's still my best friend.

I purposely haven't said much about my twelve-year-old daughter, Madeline. She lives in the suburbs of San Francisco with Debra. She appears happy and well adjusted. I see her every week for dinner and every other weekend she stays with me in the city. The things I love best about her are her sense of humor and the fact that she lets disappointments roll off her back. She takes everything in stride, so nothing gets to her very much. I wish I could be more like Madeline. I don't think a father could be more proud and I make it a point to tell her this every time I see her. And I know every father thinks his daughter is the most beautiful, but mine really is.

In actuality, I wrote this book for Madeline. I'd like her to read it when she gets older. I want her to know more about me, get a better understanding of who I am and what I went through. My wish is that she'll realize I worked very hard not treat her the way my parents treated me. It's cliché, but I want her to have what I never did, at least from an emotional perspective. And no, I never once raised a hand to her, even when she helped herself to the contents of my wallet or convinced Lynn summer camp was cancelled so she could hang out with her all day. Instead we talked about it, and she never did it again. I'm not sure what smacking her in the head would have accomplished, except make her write a book like this.

My old girlfriend, Jacqui, is still in my life. We reconnected right before my divorce. She was working on cruise ships seeing the world and had just returned to Philadelphia to live. Both her parents had died and she was heading for her second divorce, but we felt like long lost family and since have spoken and visited on a regular basis. And best of all, she didn't get divorced but remained married to this Scottish-skirt-wearing bastard named Bobby who I really think is great. I hope she will be in my life forever because she adds something very special to it.

As for me, I am anxiously awaiting my marriage to Lynn. We live in San Francisco, my twentieth year in the city. We have two cats and two dogs all antagonizing one another and helping to destroy our home, one gnawed piece of furniture and carpet stain at a time. I started my own marketing-PR firm which is floundering around and am in search of a new radio station that will let me screw up on the air a few hours a week. I also still volunteer at San Quentin State Prison, not as a teacher, but in a program designed to help inmates about to be released to successfully reintegrate into society and not re-offend. I truly admire the inmates involved who co-run the program, the outside volunteers and the incarcerated men. I wish working to help them could be my full time occupation. I feel it's the most important thing I do in life.

I still take my cocktail of antidepressants and mood stabilizers, see my therapist once a week and my psychopharmacologist every three months. So far I think I'm on the best medication combination ever, with the least side effects and the most positive control over my depression and mania. Sporadically I attend group meetings, when I feel like I want to be around my own kind, but often find it hard to relate to certain people who prefer disability to a little discipline.

I think there is a time and place for self-discipline, like sitting down and writing a book. Or, quitting smoking. Maybe even getting back in good physical condition. But telling a depressed person to "snap out of it" has nothing to do with self-discipline. The self-discipline I'm referring to is trying to hang on to the belief that the seemingly bottomless depression won't last forever and that the doctor will find the right mix of medications. And then, learning to live with the uncomfortable side effects of "feeling better."

I am low man on the bipolar totem pole. I had a parent who was reluctant to treat me for fear of exposing herself, another who didn't want to pay for it because "he was sick of being nickeled and dimed to death" and a litany of doctors with violent reactions to dry cleaning fluids and a fear of getting hit by a lightning bolt if they didn't follow the

1946 version of *The Physicians' Desk Reference*. I've been beaten, humiliated, misdiagnosed, under and over medicated, suicidal, in denial and constantly on trial. But I'm still here. It amazes me to this day. I can see my obituary now: "He could sing. He could dance. Now he doesn't need that bottle of Lorazepam in his pants."

Oh, and I heard Dr. Face Melt passed away. I don't know where they buried him, but I hear when you visit his grave you have to pre-pay and then submit it to insurance yourself for reimbursement.

www.ingramcontent.com/pod-product-compliance
Lightning Source LLC
Chambersburg PA
CBHW060254290526
45789CB00001B/329